IRISH R/
TRACTION

G000166865

SECOND EDITION

The Complete Guide to all NIR and IR Locomotives & Coaching
Stock together with Loco Diagrams and Distance Tables

Peter Jones

Published by Metro Enterprises Ltd., 48 Southcliffe Drive, Baildon, Shipley,
West Yorkshire, BD17 5QX.

Printed by Bayliss Printing Company of Worksop, Knight & Forster of Leeds
and Icon Impressions of Bacup.

ISBN 0 947773 15 0

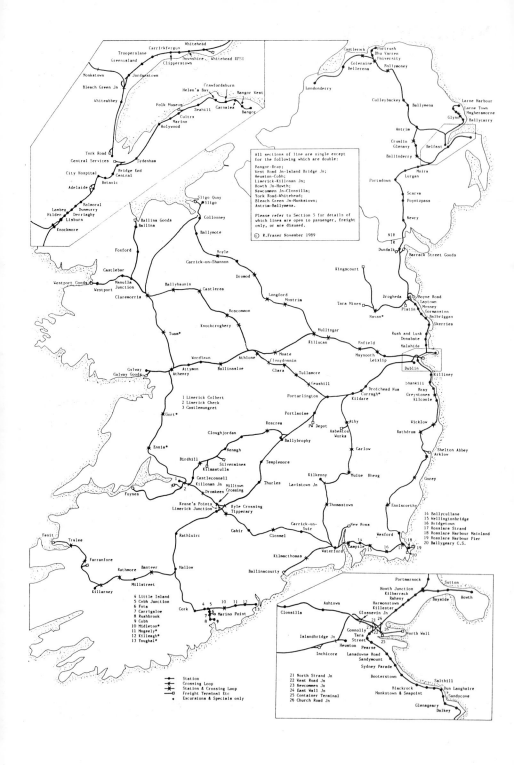

All sections of line are single except
for the following which are double:

Bangor-Bray;
West Road Jn-Island Bridge Jn;
Heuston-Cobh;
Limerick-Killonan Jn;
Howth Jn-Howth;
Newcomen Jn-Clonsilla;
York Road-Whitehead;
Bleach Green Jn-Monkstown;
Antrim-Ballymena.

Please refer to Section 5 for details of
which lines are open to passenger, freight
only, or are disused.

© R.Fraser November 1989

INTRODUCTION

Since the publication of the first edition of "Irish Railways Traction & Travel" in September 1987, the interest in the modern day scene on both Northern Ireland Railways and Irish Rail has grown significantly. This has resulted in an increased demand by enthusiasts, for greater information relating to the locomotive and rolling stock fleets of both railway companies. The purpose of this second edition is to update the reader with current events and to expand on areas not previously covered in the first edition.

Information is updated to that available at the beginning of November 1989.

GENERAL NOTES

The current Irish railway network is operated by two companies, Iarnrod Eireann (Irish Rail–IR) in the Republic and Northern Ireland Railways (NIR) in the Northern Counties. Iarnrod Eireann is a subsidiary company of Coras Iompair Eireann (CIE), the Irish transport holding company which itself operated the service in the Republic via its railway division until 2nd February 1987.

Included in this book is a full list of all classes of locomotives that were included in the CIE renumbering scheme of 1972 and all NIR classes of locomotives which have seen service since that year. Individual locomotive details (where available records permit) are given, including notes regarding final disposal where a locomotive is no longer in traffic. It should be noted that certain CIE locomotives that were withdrawn from service prior to 1972, but whose class were included in the 1972 renumbering scheme, are included so as to give a complete listing for each class. Photographs are included of most of the classes of locomotives described in the text.

Included in this edition for the first time is a full list of all IR, CIE, Northern Counties Commitee, Great Northern Railway of Ireland , Ulster Transport Authority and NIR diesel and petrol driven multiple units built since 1933, together with individual vehicle details (where available records permit), including notes regarding final disposal (where known) where a vehicle no longer exists. Also included for the first time are similar details of the push/pull sets to which many CIE dmus were subsequently converted. Many types are illustrated to complement the text.

A full current coaching stock fleetlist is given for both IR and NIR, together with brief technical details. Many types are illustrated to complement the text.

A full list of current passenger train identification numbers is given for both companies, together with details of the planned locomotive workings (diagrams) for those trains which are locomotive hauled. A schedule shows how both these and non-passenger train identification numbers are derived on the Irish Rail system.

Mileage tables are included for all routes which are still open to either passenger or other traffic on both systems. Also included are tables of routes which although "closed" may still see very occasional traffic. Details of permanent speed restrictions and their locations are quoted in order to assist readers whose interest lies in the field of train timing.

Northern Ireland Railways operate all internal passenger services within Northern Ireland and shares the cross border passenger services with Irish Rail. Freight services running exclusively in Northern Ireland are also operated by NIR, but cross border freight services are operated by Irish Rail. Irish Rail operates all internal passenger and freight services within the Republic.

ROVER TICKETS

Railway enthusiasts may find rover tickets very useful for travel in Ireland. At the time of writing the following are available (prices as at November 1989, but subject to revision):

Irish Rail

8 Day IR Rambler Ticket: Cost I£52 Adult, I£26 Child, Standard Class Only. 8 days unlimited travel within a fixed 15 day period.

15 Day IR Rambler Ticket: Cost I£77 Adult, I£38 Child, Standard Class Only. 15 days unlimited travel within a fixed 30 day period.

1 Day DART Rover: Cost I£2.50 Adult, I£1.25 Child, Standard Class Only. One days unlimited travel in the Dublin Suburban area bounded by Balbriggan, Kilcoole, Howth and Maynooth.

Northern Ireland Railways

7 Day All–Line Runabout Ticket (Summer Only): Cost £25 Adult, £12.50 Child. Seven days unlimited travel on all NIR services.

Both Systems

8 Day Irish Rover Ticket: Cost I£65 (£55) Adult. Standard Class Only. 8 days unlimited travel on both IR & NIR rail networks within a fixed 15 day period.

The above tickets cannot be obtained in the Britain and are only available from the relevant operator.

RAIL ENQUIRY OFFICES

Northern Ireland Railways

InterCity Travel Centre, 17 Wellington Place, Belfast, BT1 6GB.	0232 230671
Travel Centre, Larne Harbour.	0574 70517
Travel & Information Centre, Central Station, Belfast, BT1 3TB	0232 230310

Irish Rail

Passenger Enquiries Dublin Area	Dublin 366222
Connolly Station, Amiens Street, Dublin 1.	Dublin 742941
Heuston Station, Dublin 8.	Dublin 771871

SHIPPING SERVICES

The following is a list shipping services and their operators between the UK and Ireland. Further details may be obtained directly from the operators at the addresses/telephone numbers given below.

Route	Operator	Scheduled Crossing Time
Swansea–Cork*	Swansea Cork Ferries	10 hours.
Fishguard–Rosslare	Sealink (UK) Ltd.	3½ hours.
Pembroke–Rosslare	B & I Steam Packet Co.	4 hours.
Holyhead–Dun Laoghaire	Sealink (UK) Ltd.	3½ hours.
Holyhead–Dublin	B & I Steam Packet Co.	3½ hours.
Liverpool–Dun Laoghaire†	Sealink (UK) Ltd.	8 or 9 hours.
Liverpool–Belfast	Belfast Ferries Ltd.	9 hours.
Stranraer–Larne	Sealink (UK) Ltd.	2½ hours.
Cairnryan–Larne	P & O European Ferries	2¼ hours.

* Service currently suspended until further notice.
† Service to be withdrawn early in 1990.

ADDRESSES & TELEPHONE NUMBERS

Sealink (UK) Ltd.

Fishguard Harbour, Fishguard, Dyfed, SA64 0BX.	0348 872881
Turkeyshore Road, Holyhead, Gwynedd, LL65 2DD.	0407 2304
Sea Terminal, Stranraer, Dumfries & Galloway, DG9 8EJ.	0776 2262
33–37 Castle Lane, Belfast, County Antrim, BT1 5DB.	0232 327525
P.O. Box 29, Victoria Station, London, SW1V 1JC.	01 834 8122
Travel Centre, 28 Cross Street, Manchester, M2 3NH.	
Charter House, Park Street, Ashford, Kent, TN24 8EX.	0233 47047
Recorded Information Service.	0233 610341
Prestel.	Page 545040

B & I Steam Packet Co.
150/1 New Bond Street, London, W1Y 0AQ.

01 734 4681
01 734 7512

Belfast Ferries Ltd.
47 Donegal Quay, Belfast, BT1 3ED.
Brocklebank Dock, Bootle, Liverpool, L20 1DB.

0232 320634
051 922 6234

P & O European Ferries
Passenger Terminal, The Harbour, Larne, BT40 1AQ.
Passenger Terminal, Cairnryan, Stranraer, DG9 8RF.

0574 74321
05812 276

ACCOMMODATION

Unlike British Rail, there are no overnight long distance passenger services and accommodation must be found for those who wish to visit Ireland for longer than a day. A list of reasonably priced Bed & Breakfast accommodation which can be recommended by the author, and are situated near to main railway stations, is included as an appendix at the rear of this book.

NOTES APPLICABLE TO ALL ROLLING STOCK

Notes of a non general nature are given under the appropriate company and type of stock.

General

Class details and dimensions are shown in imperial units with the metric equivalents (with the exception of weights, 1 ton ê 1.016 tonnes) given in parentheses.

Unlike BR, vehicles are not allocated to specific depots for maintenance purposes. All maintenance work other than daily servicing is done at Inchicore (IR) or York Road/Central Services Depot (NIR).

Dates To Traffic

The date shown is the date or month the vehicle was officially accepted into traffic. This should not be confused with the arrival/delivery date as each vehicle can be subject to a series of test runs and examinations over a period of time prior to final acceptance. Depending on the sucess or otherwise of these tests/examinations and other factors e.g. Holidays, Industrial Disputes etc., the time interval between delivery and acceptance could run into weeks or months. Information is given as far as available official records permit, especially in the case of the older vehicles, where few, if any, records still exist.

Date Stopped

Note: These dates are shown only for locomotives as data is not available for multiple unit stock.

The date shown is the date that the locomotive last worked in traffic prior to failure or recall to works for storage. The dates were obtained from the individual locomotive record cards and then checked against the daily locomotive log maintained at the locomotive control. Many errors were found during the initial research e.g. dates transposed between locomotives, numbers transposed from page to page, entries omitted etc., especially for those locomotives which were shown stopped over several years before they were finally written off. Hopefully these have now been eliminated and the correct dates shown.

Date Withdrawn

This is the date or month that each vehicle was finally written off the Company's books and/or sanctioned for scrapping. This date may be several years after the vehicle was stopped (see above), or only a few days, depending on the circumstances. e.g. A vehicle may succumb to a major failure, and then be used as a source of spare parts. Such a vehicle would still be shown as officially in stock until such time as it is deemed to be of no further value, when it would be withdrawn/sanctioned for scrap. If this occurs on the first few vehicles to be stopped within a class, then the withdrawal date will be significantly later than the stopped date, but if it should occur on the final few vehciles of a class, then obviously the spare parts would be of less value and hence the withdrawal date will be much nearer the stopped date. In a few isolated cases vehicles have been withdrawn whilst still in traffic, e.g. It may have been decided to eliminate the final few vehicles of a particular class as surplus to requirements. In such cases a vehicle may not have been taken out of traffic until it suffered a failure, which may be some time after the official withdrawal date. In some instances vehicles have been stopped following failure, but kept reasonably intact so that they may be repaired for further service should the need arise at some future date. This occurred with the 101 class locomotives of CIE, which were stopped over the period 1969 to 1978, but retained until sanctioned for withdrawal in 1984 as locomotives of 201 class were then surplus and set aside for this purpose. During 1986 many 071 class locomotives were found to have serious bogie defects which necessitated their being taken out of traffic for repairs. This resulted in several 201 class locomotives being temporarily returned to traffic to cover the resultant shortage of locomotives. All locomotive withdrawal dates for CIE/IR have been extracted from memos issued by the General Manager authorising the writing off of a locomotive from the company's books.

Locomotive Fittings and Details

Individual locomotive fittings are shown against each locomotive number. For a locomotive no longer in traffic, the fittings shown are as at the date the locomotive was finally stopped. This is because certain fittings have been removed from redundant locomotives for further use in servicable locomotives and is particularly true with regard to the CAWS. equipment fitted in each locomotive cab. As all locomotives except CIE 301–5 and 601–3 were fitted with vacuum brakes when new, this is not shown as an individual characteristic against each locomotive.

The following abbreviations are used to denote the various fittings:

A–Fitted with train air brakes in addition to vacuum brakes.
E–Fitted with electric train heating equipment.
M–Fitted with multiple working facility (see locomotive class headings for restrictions).
N–Fitted with push/pull facility (former CIE system).
O–Fitted with push/pull facility (with suitably equipped NIR vehicles only).
P–Fitted with Mark 3 push/pull facility. (with suitably equipped IR vehicles only).
R–Fitted with NIR train radio.
S–Fitted with CAWS. (Continuous Automatic Warning System) for operating over the CTC (Centralised Traffic Control) system.
X–Fitted with engine bonnet extension.

No locomotives except the NIR 101 class are fitted with any form of train heating equipment, train heat being provided by boiler or generator vans included in the train formation.

Cut Up/Disposal Date

This is the approximate date, given to the nearest month, that a vehicle was finally broken up for scrap or disposed of for a reason other than further use. (e.g. Many multiple units were consigned to a tip for burial due to asbestos contamination). Certain information on this front has eluded the author and any information that readers may posess would be welcome. Such missing information is denoted by a ? symbol in the vehicle tables. Withdrawn vehicles shown in the text with this column blank are currently stored awaiting further instructions.

Cut Up/Store/Disposal Location

This is the last known location at the time of going to press of a stopped/ withdrawn vehicle. In the case of a vehicle no longer in existence (or buried due to asbestos contamination) a date is shown in the previous column and the location given is the location where the vehicle was cut up or buried. In other cases the vehicle is still extant at the location shown. Preserved locomotives are shown at their current location and are indicated by (P). Certain information on this front has eluded the author and any information that readers may posess would be welcome. Such missing information is denoted by a ? symbol in the vehicle tables.

Diesel Railcar & Multiple Unit Stock

All railcar & multiple unit details relate to their original configuration as railcars/multiple units unless otherwise stated. All third class vehicles were re–designated standard class from June 1956 following the UIC decision to abolish the ertswhile second class.

All vehicles are to be assumed to be of Open seating layout unless otherwise stated.

All vehicle superstructure dimensions are given over body.

Details of modifications and dates when carried out are given as notes where appropriate and/or information is available.

In all subsections power cars are listed first, followed by trailers. This is relevant where duplication of numbers between power cars and trailers exists.

ABBREVIATIONS

The following abbreviations are used throughout this book:

(A)	Asbestos Contaminated Vehicle, buried rather than cut up.
AEC	Associated Engine Company.
BR	British Rail.
BREL	British Rail Engineering Limited.
CIE	Coras Iompair Eireann.
DART	Dublin Area Rapid Transit.
F	First Class seats.
GSR	Great Southern Railway.
GNR(I)	Great Northern Railway (Ireland).
I	InterCity sector (NIR)
IR	Irish Rail (Iarnrod Eireann).
NIR	Northern Ireland Railways.
NCC	Northern Counties Committee.
(P)	Preserved
PW	Permanent Way.
S	Standard Class seats or Suburban Sector (NIR).(see context)
SCG	Self Changing Gears Ltd.
T	Third Class seats.
UTA	Ulster Transport Authority
hp	horsepower.
kN	kilonewtons.
kW	kilowatts.
lbf	pounds force.
lb/hr	pounds per hour.
mph	miles per hour.
kph	kilometers per hour.
rpm	revolutions per minute.

ACKNOWLEDGEMENTS

The author would like to thank both Irish Rail and Northern Ireland Railways for their help in the production of this book, and in particular the following for their help in answering queries:

Northern Ireland Railways

Denis Grimshaw, David McKeown, Chris McMurray, Frank Dunlop.

Irish Rail

Cyril Ferris, Mary Linehan, Marie Butterley, Charlie Rowley, John Huber, Tommy Green, Paddy O'Sullivan, John Keely, Vincent Connolly, Val Hogan, Reggie Morris, Fran Greene, John Power, Mick Walsh, Joe Clarke, John Burke, Tony Fay, Paddy Donnelly, Ted Phillips, Larry Reid, Tony Whalley, Dessie Kavanagh, Derek O' Grady, Seamus O'Reilly, Eddie Billings, Jack Phelan, Brendan O'Byrne, Bernie Colman, Harry O'Donnell, Joe O'Ryan, Terry Long, Pat Mackay, Harry O'Brien, Colin Allen, Mickey Moore, Frank Shine, Dan Renehan, Arthur Hanlon, Don O' Mahoney, Eddie Delaney, Brendan Flynn, Sean Carter, Jack Ahern, Michael Nugent, Val Ford.

The author is also grateful to the following enthusiasts for their valuable contributions: David Parks, David Hegarty, Jonathan Allen, William Watson, Alan McFerran, Michael McMahon.

SECTION 1 – IRISH RAIL STOCK LIST.
BRIEF HISTORY

Iarnrod Eireann (Irish Rail) came into existence on 2nd February 1987 when the original state owned national transport authority, Coras Iompair Eireann, was split up into three subsidiary companies. Of these three, Iarnrod Eireann takes over responsibility for the operation of all rail services within the Irish Republic, Bus Atha Cliath is responsible for Dublin bus services and Bus Eireann for other bus services.

CIE was itself formed on 1st January 1945 when the former Great Southern Railway and the Dublin United Transport Company were amalgamated under the terms of the 1944 Transport Act. CIE was then nationalised under the 1950 Transport Act, and absorbed the lines south of the border of the former Great Northern Railway (Ireland) in 1958 when this was divided between the CIE and the then Ulster Transport Authority by the Great Northern Railway Act of that year.

LOCOMOTIVE CLASSIFICATION

The diesel locomotive fleet of CIE was formerly classified by letters which prefixed locomotive numbers. This letter gave an indication of the power output of the locomotive (A being the highest, and so on), but was eventually dropped in 1972 in favour of the present number only scheme. However, many departments within Irish Rail still refer to locomotives by their former letter classifications, and therefore these are shown in brackets in class headings following the current classification. (n.b. 201 class locomotives are still known as "C" class, their original designation, although they were reclassified "B" after re-engining.)

071 class locomotives never received a letter classification as they were delivered after the scheme was discontinued.

LOCOMOTIVES
001 CLASS (A)   Co–Co

Built: 1955–56 by Metropolitan Vickers at Dukinfield Works, Manchester.
Original Engine: Crossley HSTV8 of 1200 hp (896 kW) at 625 rpm.
Rebuilt: 1968–71 by CIE at Inchicore Works, Dublin.
Current Engine: General Motors 12–645E of 1325 hp (989 kW) at 800 rpm. (* 12–645E of 1650 hp (1231 kW) at 900 rpm.)
Transmission: Electric.
Traction Motors: Metropolitan Vickers MV137CW.
Max. Tractive Effort: 46000 lbf (205 kN).
Cont. Tractive Effort: 18000 lbf (80 kN) at 21½ mph.
Power At Rail: 1032 hp (770 kW). (*1295 hp (966 kW)).
Weight: 82 tons.
Length Over Buffers: 51 ft (15.54 m)
Wheel Diameter: 3 ft 2 in (965 mm)
Maximum Speed: 75 mph (* 80 mph).
Works Numbers: 887–946 in order. All works plates show built 1955.

Loco No.	Fittings	Date to Traffic	Date Rebuilt	Date Stopped	Date Withdrawn	Month Cut	Cut Up/Store Location
001	S	27.09.55	30.03.71				
002	S	29.09.55	17.12.70				
003	S	27.09.55	10.03.71				
004		01.10.55	19.02.71	23.07.79	13.04.84	09.84	Inchicore Works.
005	S	06.10.55	21.09.71				
006		03.10.55	12.11.71	09.09.83	05.10.84		Inchicore Barrier.
007	S	14.10.55	06.07.71				
008		18.10.55	30.07.70	23.10.73	05.10.77	?	Inchicore Works.
009	S	18.10.55	08.10.70				

010		20.10.55	26.10.70	20.12.78	13.04.84	09.84	Inchicore Works.
011	S	24.10.55	01.02.71				
012	S	28.02.56	10.06.71				
013	S	30.11.55	13.01.71				
014	S	06.12.55	11.02.71				
015	S	24.12.55	20.05.71				
016	S	20.12.55	02.12.70				
017	S	07.01.56	04.11.70				
018	S	16.01.56	16.07.71				
019	S	26.01.56	28.09.70				
020	S	01.02.56	31.08.70				
021	S	05.02.56	01.04.71				
022	S	19.02.56	19.05.70				
023	S	19.02.56	18.06.71				
024	S	23.02.56	01.09.71	25.04.86	28.01.87		Inchicore Works.
025	S	03.03.56	17.07.70				
026	S	10.03.56	25.11.71				
027*	S	06.03.56	24.06.70				
028		16.03.56	04.05.70	09.02.84	05.10.84		Inchicore Works.
029	SA	23.03.56	24.04.70	13.07.88			Inchicore Depot.
030	S	19.03.56	30.01.70				
031	S	11.04.56	22.09.71				
032		29.03.56	06.02.70	12.03.83	05.10.84		Inchicore Barrier.
033	S	29.03.56	13.03.70				
034	S	29.03.56	09.12.69	25.06.86	28.01.87		Inchicore Depot.
035	S	15.04.56	20.08.69				
036*	S	17.04.56	01.12.69				
037		28.04.56	02.03.70	15.11.83	05.10.84		Inchicore Barrier.
038	S	24.04.56	17.04.71				
039	S	14.05.56	23.07.69				
040	S	30.04.56	28.10.69	01.06.88			Inchicore Works.
041		08.05.56	22.07.69	18.01.83	05.10.84		Inchicore Barrier.
042	S	19.05.56	20.07.69				
043	S	06.06.56	15.09.71	17.06.88			Inchicore Works.
044		19.05.56	29.05.70	31.10.83	05.10.84		Inchicore Barrier.
045		30.05.56	04.11.69	08.03.84	05.10.84		Inchicore Works.
046*		31.05.56	10.04.70	21.04.79	14.01.80	?	Inchicore Works.
047	S	15.06.56	24.10.69				
048	S	23.06.56	01.10.69				
049	S	23.06.56	10.09.69				
050	S	31.07.56	28.09.71	20.09.86	28.01.87		Inchicore Works.
051	S	16.06.56	04.10.69				
052	S	12.07.56	06.12.69				
053	S	26.06.56	18.08.71				
054*	S	23.06.56	04.11.71				
055	S	01.08.56	01.07.70				
056*	S	23.08.56	10.11.69				
057	S	08.09.56	27.03.70				
058	S	20.09.56	12.05.68				
059*	S	20.10.56	22.07.68	29.04.86	28.01.87		Inchicore Barrier.
060	S	09.01.57	15.01.70	09.12.83	05.10.84		Inchicore Works.

004 was hijacked, derailed and burned at Goraghwood on 23.07.79.

008 was bombed at Meigh on 23.10.73. Some remains are still on site.

010 collided with NIR vehicles 69, 768 and 742 at Lisburn whilst working the 1100 Belfast Central to Dublin Connolly "Enterprise Express" on 20.12.78.

029 is stored awaiting a decision on it's future following fire damage.

040 is stored awaiting a decision on it's future following collision damage.

043 is stored awaiting a decision on it's future following fire damage.

046 was bombed at at milepost 65¼ (Killeen Bridge) between Dublin and Belfast on 21.04.79.

071 CLASS

Co–Co

Built: 1976 by General Motors, La Grange, Illinois, U.S.A.
Engine: General Motors 12–645E3B of 2475 hp (1845 kW) at 900 rpm.
Transmission: Electric.
Traction Motors: General Motors D77B.
Max. Tractive Effort: 55100 lbf (245 kN).
Cont. Tractive Effort: 46850 lbf (209 kN) at 15.1 mph.
Power At Rail: 1823 hp (1360 kW).
Weight: 99 tons.
Length Over Buffers: 57 ft (17.37 m).
Wheel Diameter: 3 ft 4 in (1016 mm).
Maximum Speed: 90 mph.
Works Numbers: 713736–713753 in order.
Multiple Working: Within class & with classes 121, 141, 181 & NIR 111. However, the use of this facility is prohibited by IR.

Loco No.	Fittings	Date to Traffic
071	SAM	30.05.77
072	SAM	01.06.77
073	SAM	02.06.77
074	SAM	04.06.77
075	SAM	02.06.77
076	SAM	24.05.77
077	SAM	06.06.77
078	SAM	30.05.77
079	SAM	25.05.77
080	SAM	30.05.77
081	SAM	27.05.77
082	SAM	23.05.77
083	SAM	29.06.77
084	SAM	30.05.77
085	SAM	25.05.77
086	SAM	14.06.77
087	SAM	26.05.77
088	SAM	06.07.77

All locomotives were built new with a power reduction system (similar to slow speed control), but this was seldom used and has now been isolated on most locomotives. Due to a weight restriction these locomotives are banned from the bridge at milepost 156 over the River Moy on the line between Manulla Junction and Ballina.

101 CLASS (B)

A1A–A1A

Built: 1956–57 The Birmingham Railway Carriage & Wagon Company at Smethwick.
Engine: Sulzer 6LDA28 of 960 hp (716 kW) at 710 rpm.
Transmission: Electric.
Traction Motors: Metropolitan Vickers MV137CW.
Max. Tractive Effort: 41800 lbf (186 kN).
Cont. Tractive Effort: 16900 lbf (76 kN) at 16 mph.
Power At Rail:
Weight: 75.45 tons.
Length Over Buffers: 47 ft 8 in (14.53 m).
Wheel Diameter: 3 ft 1½ in (953 mm).
Maximum Speed: 75 mph.
Works Numbers: Not allocated.

Loco No.	Date to Traffic	Date Stopped	Month Withdrawn	Month Cut	Cut Up/Store Location
101	09.04.56	06.05.74	04.84	03.87	North Wall Point Yard
102	04.08.56	03.10.74	04.84	03.87	North Wall Point Yard
103	13.08.56	17.11.77	04.84		Inchicore Works (P)

▲ B101 & B102 stabled at Thurles in 1971. *Herbert Richards*

▼ B114 stands outside the workshops at Inchicore in 1968. This locomotive is to be restored by Westrail.

Herbert Richards

104	30.08.56	15.07.74	04.84	01.87	North Wall Point Yard
105	17.09.56	22.11.77	04.84	03.87	North Wall Point Yard
106	08.11.56	07.02.78	04.84	12.86	North Wall Point Yard
107	25.02.57	25.05.77	04.84	02.87	North Wall Point Yard
108	16.04.57	10.01.73	04.84	01.87	North Wall Point Yard
109	19.06.57	20.01.75	04.84	02.87	North Wall Point Yard
110	13.07.57	15.11.77	04.84	04.87	North Wall Point Yard
111	15.10.57	13.05.69	04.84	04.87	North Wall Point Yard
112	23.12.57	27.07.73	04.84	02.87	North Wall Point Yard

103 has been preserved by Westrail.

113 CLASS (B)   Bo–Bo

Built: 1950–51 by CIE at Inchicore Works, Dublin.
Engine: Sulzer 6LDA28 of 960 hp (716 kW) at 710 rpm.
Transmission: Electric.
Traction Motors: Metropolitan Vickers MV137CW.
Max. Tractive Effort: 46000 lbf (205 kN).
Cont. Tractive Effort: 23000 lbf (102 kN) at 9½ mph.
Power At Rail:
Weight: 80 tons.
Length Over Buffers: 47 ft 8 in (14.53 m).
Wheel Diameter: 3 ft 8 in (1118 mm).
Maximum Speed: 55 mph.
Works Numbers: Not allocated.
Note: The engines in these locomotives were originally rated at 915 hp (683 kW) at 750 rpm, but were uprated in 1956 to the figures shown above. These locomotives were originally fitted with Spanner Swirlyflow train heating boilers, these being removed upon the introduction of steam heating vans.

Loco No.	Date to Traffic	Date Stopped	Date Withdrawn	Cut Up/Store Location
113	.04.50	07.01.75	18.12.77	Inchicore Works (P).
114	.10.51	30.08.71	18.12.77	Inchicore Works (P).

113 has been preserved by the Great Southern Railway Preservation Society.

114 has been preserved by Westrail.

These locomotives originally carried the numbers 1100 and 1101 respectively but were renumbered in 1957 as shown above. 113 was out of service from 05.01.72 until 11.10.74 when modifications to the braking system were undertaken and the locomotive reinstated. 114 was similarly treated on 04.12.74 but never returned to service.

121 CLASS(B)   Bo–Bo

Built: 1960 by General Motors, La Grange, Illinois, USA.
Engine: General Motors 8–567CR of 950 hp (709 kW) at 835 rpm. (* 8–B645E of 1100 hp (821 kW) at 900 rpm).
Transmission: Electric.
Traction Motors: General Motors D47.
Max. Tractive Effort: 35000 lbf (156 kN).
Cont. Tractive Effort: 30400 lbf (135 kN) at 8 mph (* 26400 lbf (118 kN) at 11 mph.
Power At Rail: 709 hp (529 kW) (* 810 hp (604 kW)).
Weight: 64 tons.
Length Over Buffers: 39 ft 10¼ in (12.15 m).
Wheel Diameter: 3 ft 4 in (1016 mm).
Maximum Speed: 77 mph.
Works Numbers: 26271–26285 in order.
Multiple Working: Within class & with classes 071, 141, 181 & NIR 111.

Loco No.	Fittings	Date to Traffic	Month Re-engined	Date Stopped	Cut Up/ Store Location	Notes
121	SAMN	20.02.61				
122	SAMP	04.03.61				
123	SAMP	08.04.61				
124	SAMP	29.03.61				
125	SAMN	29.03.61		06.03.86	Inchicore Depot	
126*	SAMP	20.02.61	07.88			Engine ex 213.
127*	SAMP	14.03.61	06.87			Engine ex 205.
128*	SAMP	20.02.61	10.88			Engine ex 192.
129*	SAMN	20.03.61	.84			Engine ex 204.
130	SAMP	20.02.61				
131	SAMP	20.02.61				
132	SAMP	05.04.61				
133	SAMN	16.03.61				
134	SAMN	20.02.61				
135	SAMN	20.02.61				

121 was fitted with an 8–B645E engine ex 221 from 02.87 to 12.88, but is now fitted with an 8–567CR engine once more.

125 suffered a major electrical fire on 06.03.86 and has now been partially cannibalised for spare parts. No decision has yet been made on the future of this locomotive.

141 CLASS (B)   Bo–Bo

Built: 1962 by General Motors, La Grange, Illinois, USA.
Engine: General Motors 8–567CR of 950 hp (709 kW) at 835 rpm. (* 8–B645E of 1100 hp (821 kW) at 900 rpm).
Transmission: Electric.
Traction Motors: General Motors D57.
Max. Tractive Effort: 37500 lbf (167 kN).
Cont. Tractive Effort: 27000 lbf (120 kN) at 9 mph (* 26400 lbf (118 kN) at 11 mph.
Power At Rail: 709 hp (529 kW) (* 810 hp (604 kW)).
Weight: 67 tons.
Length Over Buffers: 44 ft 0½ in (13.42 m).
Wheel Diameter: 3 ft 4 in (1016 mm).
Maximum Speed: 80 mph.
Works Numbers: 27467–27503 in order.
Multiple Working: Within class & with classes 071, 121, 181 & NIR 111.

Loco No.	Fittings	Date to Traffic	Month Re–engined	Notes
141	SAM	13.12.62		
142	SAM	03.12.62		
143	SAM	20.06.63		
144	SAM	14.01.63		
145*	SAM	10.01.63	03.87	Engine ex 219.
146	SAM	14.12.62		
147	SAM	14.12.62		
148	SAM	08.12.62		
149	SAM	14.12.62		
150	SAM	03.12.62		
151	SAM	08.12.62		
152	SAM	03.12.62		
153	SAM	13.12.62		
154*	SAM	11.12.62	02.89	Engine ex 221.
155	SAM	03.12.62		
156	SAM	03.12.62		
157*	SAM	05.12.62	03.86	Engine ex 220.
158	SAM	03.12.62		
159	SAM	13.12.62		
160	SAM	08.12.62		

161	SAM	06.12.62		
162	SAM	05.12.62		
163*	SAM	05.12.62	09.86	Engine ex 215.
164	SAM	05.12.62		
165	SAM	19.12.62		
166	SAM	14.12.62		
167*	SAM	13.12.62	05.87	Engine ex 214.
168	SAM	08.12.62		
169	SAM	28.12.62		
170*	SAM	19.12.62	03.86	Engine ex 233.
171	SAM	04.01.63		
172	SAM	28.12.62		
173	SAM	21.12.62		
174	SAM	21.12.62		
175*	SAM	04.01.63	.88	Engine ex 202.
176	SAM	21.12.62		
177	SAM	28.12.62		

The engine in 154 came from 221 via 121.

175 was equipped with the engine ex 225 from 11.86 to .88.

181 CLASS (B)   Bo–Bo

Built: 1966 by General Motors, La Grange, Illinois, USA.
Engine: General Motors 8–645E of 1100 hp (821 kW) at 900 rpm.
Transmission: Electric.
Traction Motors: General Motors D77.
Max. Tractive Effort: 37500 lbf (167 kN).
Cont. Tractive Effort: 26400 lbf (118 kN) at 11 mph.
Power At Rail: 810 hp (604 kW).
Weight: 67 tons.
Length Over Buffers: 44 ft 0½ in (13.42 m).
Wheel Diameter: 3 ft 4 in (1016 mm).
Maximum Speed: 80 mph.
Works Numbers: 31248–31259 in order.
Multiple Working: Within class & with classes 071, 121, 141 & NIR 111.

Loco No.	Fittings	Date to Traffic
181	SAM	03.12.66
182	SAM	28.11.66
183	SAM	27.11.66
184	SAM	29.11.66
185	SAM	08.12.66
186	SAM	29.11.66
187	SAM	28.11.66
188	SAM	28.11.66
189	SAM	02.12.66
190	SAM	03.12.66
191	SAM	03.12.66
192	SAM	06.12.66

Cover Photograph Captions

Front: 101 and 104 at Belfast Central on 10th September 1989.   *Andrew Marshall*

Rear: 121 Class No. B135 at Athenry with a Dublin to Galway service during May 1971.
Jonathan Allen

201 CLASS (C)   Bo–Bo

Built: 1956–57 by Metropolitan Vickers at Dukinfield Works, Manchester.
Original Engine: Crossley ESTV8 of 550 hp (410 kW) at 1000 rpm.
Rebuilt: 1969–80 by CIE at Inchicore Works, Dublin.
Current Engine: General Motors 8–B645E of 1100 hp (821 kW) at 900 rpm.
Transmission: Electric.
Traction Motors: Metropolitan Vickers MV137CW.
Max. Tractive Effort: 34440 lbf (153 kN).
Cont. Tractive Effort:
Power At Rail: 842 hp (629 kW).
Weight: 61.5 tons.
Length Over Buffers: 42 ft (12.80 m).
Wheel Diameter: 3 ft 2 in (965 mm).
Maximum Speed: 80 mph.
Works Numbers: 947–980 in order. All works plates show built 1956.

Note: 233 and 234 were re–engined with Maybach MD650 engines of 980 hp (731 kW) at 1200 rpm on 17.05.66 and 13.12.65 respectively and retained these until dates shown below.

Loco No.	Fittings	Date to Traffic	Date Rebuilt	Date Stopped	Date Withdrawn	Month Cut	Cut Up/Store Location
201	N	04.03.57	15.06.71	15.08.73	05.10.77	?	Inchicore Works.
202	N	04.03.57	21.04.72	16.07.83	05.10.84		Inchicore Barrier.
203	N	28.03.57	06.04.72	22.08.78	13.04.84		Inchicore Works.
204	N	28.03.57	20.04.71	20.11.81	13.04.84		Inchicore Works.
205	SN	03.04.57	18.09.72	28.06.85	25.09.86		Inchicore Barrier.
206	SN	12.04.57	08.09.69	16.08.84	25.09.86		Inchicore Works.
207	N	03.04.57	24.03.72	19.11.79	13.04.84		Inchicore Works.
208	SN	17.06.57	08.07.72	30.07.85	25.09.86		Inchicore Works.
209	SN	20.05.57	19.05.72	06.10.84	25.09.86		Inchicore Works.
210	SN	16.09.57	25.04.71	30.11.83	18.09.85		Inchicore Barrier.
211	SN	20.05.57	02.06.72	15.06.85	25.09.86		Inchicore Works.
212	SN	06.07.57	05.05.72	23.05.86	25.09.86		Inchicore Works.
213	SN	11.06.57	08.02.72	29.11.86	24.11.86*£		Inchicore Works.
214	N	15.06.57	21.07.72	08.03.84	18.09.85		Inchicore Works.
215	SN	06.06.57	16.07.71	18.01.85	25.09.86		Inchicore Barrier.
216	N	11.07.57	16.11.71	04.07.85	01.04.86§		Sold to NIR.
217	SN	13.06.57	14.12.71	07.11.83	18.09.85		Inchicore Barrier.
218	N	21.06.57	21.07.72	29.11.86	24.11.86*		Sold to NIR.
219	N	01.07.57	06.10.72	26.06.85	25.09.86		Inchicore Barrier.
220	SN	24.06.57	20.12.72	01.02.85	25.09.86		Inchicore Works.
221	SN	12.08.57	14.02.72	12.08.86	25.09.86		Inchicore Works.
222	SN	13.07.57	10.03.70	30.07.86	25.09.86		Inchicore Works.
223	SN	15.07.57	17.07.72	03.06.86	25.09.86		Inchicore Works.
224	SN	10.07.57	10.09.71	12.11.84	01.04.86§		Belfast York Road.
225	SN	23.07.57	27.01.72	15.06.86	25.09.86		Inchicore Works.
226	SN	21.08.57	10.06.72	05.05.84	25.09.86		Inchicore Works.
227	SN	31.08.57	08.10.71	14.12.85	01.04.86§		Sold to NIR.
228	N	05.10.57	22.09.72	24.07.86	01.04.86§		Sold to NIR.
229	SN	12.10.57	08.03.72	23.03.84	25.09.86		Inchicore Works.
230	SN	18.11.57	18.03.71	14.12.85	01.04.86§		Sold to NIR.
231	SN	01.01.58	24.02.72	09.07.83	18.09.85		Inchicore Works.
232	SN	22.01.58	22.01.58	29.11.86	24.11.86*		Inchicore Works.
233	SN	22.01.58	29.08.80	08.03.85	25.09.86		Inchicore Works.
234	SN	22.01.58	02.07.79	04.09.85	01.04.86§		Sold to NIR.

201 was bombed at Meigh down home signal on 15.08.73 whilst working the 2215 Dundalk to Londonderry freight. Some remains are still on site, and one cab remains at Inchicore Works.

§ These six locomotives were originally sent to the NIR on a leasing arrangement, but were subsequently purchased on 1st April 1986. However, 228 was used by CIE until its despatch to Belfast on 24th July 1986. Due to 224 being found to have a bent frame after delivery, 218 was obtained as a replacement. 224 will eventually be returned to Irish Rail for final disposal.

* 213, 218 & 232 all ran in service for a few days after the official withdrawal date.

£ 213 was subsequently used as Inchicore Works pilot until February 1988.

▲ The 301 (D) Class locomotives were originally numbered 1000–1004. Here 1000 (later D301) stands at Inchicore in 1948.

J.M. Robbins

▼ G616 & G617 undergoing restoration at Mallow in September 1989.

Andrew Marshall

301 CLASS (D)

0–6–0

Built: 1946 by CIE at Inchicore Works, Dublin.
Engine: Mirrlees TLDT6 of 487 hp (363 kW) at 710 rpm.
Transmission: Electric.
Traction Motors: Two Brush traction motors.
Max. Tractive Effort: 24000 lbf (107 kN).
Cont. Tractive Effort:
Power At Rail:
Weight: 52.95 tons.
Length Over Buffers: 29 ft (8.84 m).
Wheel Diameter: 4 ft (1219 mm).
Maximum Speed: 25 mph.
Works Numbers: Not allocated.

Loco No.	Date to Traffic	Date Stopped	Date Withdrawn	Month Cut	Cut Up/Store Location
301	.46	22.06.60	17.10.76	03.77	Inchicore Works
302	.46	13.06.60	17.10.76	03.77	Inchicore Works
303	.46	09.02.70	17.10.76	03.77	Inchicore Works
304	.46	26.05.72	17.10.76	03.77	Inchicore Works
305	.46	13.06.66	17.10.76	03.77	Inchicore Works

These locomotives were originally numbered 1000 to 1004 respectively and were renumbered as shown above in 1957.

401 CLASS (E)

C

Built: 1957–58 by CIE at Inchicore Works, Dublin.
Engine: Maybach MD220 of 420 hp (313 kW) at 1600 rpm.
Transmission: Hydraulic.
Transmission Type: Mekydro KL64 Torque Converter.
Max. Tractive Effort: 21728 lbf (97 kN).
Cont. Tractive Effort:
Power At Rail: 356 hp (266 kW).
Weight: 38.8 tons.
Length Over Buffers: 29 ft 4¼ in (8.95 m).
Wheel Diameter: 3 ft 2 in (965 mm).
Maximum Speed: 25 mph.
Works Numbers: Not allocated.

Loco No.	Fittings	Date to Traffic	Date Stopped	Date Withdrawn	Month Cut	Cut Up/Store Location
401	X	10.07.57	06.08.65	12.10.77	12.77	Inchicore Works
402	X	22.10.57	10.09.75	25.02.77	04.89	Mullingar Scrapyard
403		11.11.57	18.10.76	25.02.77	04.89	Mullingar Scrapyard
404		03.01.58	16.03.77	01.06.83	.84	Inchicore Works
405		15.11.57	07.10.77	25.02.77§	.84	Inchicore Works
406	X	18.11.57	10.03.76	25.02.77	11.77	Inchicore Works
407	X	18.11.57	31.05.76	01.06.83	08.83	Mullingar Scrapyard
408		23.11.57	11.09.78	14.07.83	05.89	Mullingar Scrapyard
409		12.12.57	14.09.78	14.07.83	11.87	Mullingar Scrapyard
410	X	09.01.58	09.04.79	14.07.83	11.87	Mullingar Scrapyard
411	X	25.01.58	07.09.67	12.10.77	11.77	Inchicore Works
412		27.01.58	30.12.77	14.07.83	.84	Inchicore Works
413	X	12.02.58	10.04.75	25.02.77	01.78	Inchicore Works
414		03.02.58	12.02.77	01.06.83	.84	Inchicore Works
415	X	21.02.58	20.01.67	12.10.77	01.79	Inchicore Works
416	X	22.02.58	02.01.76	01.06.83	.84	Inchicore Works
417	X	25.03.58	05.07.67	12.10.77	01.78	Inchicore Works
418	X	20.04.58	19.10.64	01.06.83	.84	Inchicore Works
419	X	21.03.58	13.09.74	01.06.83	.84	Inchicore Works

§ 405 ran in service for some months after the official withdrawal date.

421 CLASS (E)

Built: 1962 by CIE at Inchicore Works, Dublin.
Engine: Maybach MD220 of 420 hp (313 kW) at 1600 rpm.
Transmission: Hydraulic.
Transmission Type: Mekydro KL64U Torque Converter.
Max. Tractive Effort: 23940 lbf (107 kN).
Cont. Tractive Effort:
Power At Rail: 356 hp (266 kW).
Weight: 42.8 tons.
Length Over Buffers: 31 ft 4¼ in (9.56 m).
Wheel Diameter: 3 ft 2 in (965 mm).
Maximum Speed: 25 mph.
Works Numbers: Not allocated.
Multiple Working: Within class only.

Loco No.	Fittings	Date to Traffic	Date Stopped	Date Withdrawn	Month Cut	Cut Up/Store Location
421	M	14.12.62	12.12.83	17.07.83§		Downpatrick (P).
422	M	28.09.62	08.02.83	17.07.83	10.87	Mullingar Scrapyard.
423	M	01.10.62	06.06.83	14.07.83	.84	Inchicore Works
424	M	28.09.62	09.07.79	14.07.83	10.87	Mullingar Scrapyard.
425	M	01.10.62	25.11.83	14.07.83§		Inchicore Works (P).
426	M	09.10.62	09.03.82	14.07.83	.84	Inchicore Works
427	M	22.10.62	17.11.81	14.07.83	.84	Inchicore Works
428	M	26.11.62	21.04.82	14.07.83		Tuam (P).
429	M	12.12.62	22.09.83	14.07.83§		Inchicore Works (P).
430	M	08.01.63	01.06.83	14.07.83	05.85	Attymon Junction.
431	M	25.01.63	08.12.80	14.07.83	12.88	Inchicore Works
432	M	22.01.63	15.02.83	14.07.83		Downpatrick (P).
433	M	13.04.63	24.03.83	14.07.83	12.88	Inchicore Works.
434	M	15.02.63	19.02.83	14.07.83	10.87	Mullingar Scrapyard.

§ 421, 425 & 429 ran in service for some months after the official withdrawal date.

421 & 432 have been preserved by the Downpatrick & Ardglass Railway Project, Co. Down.

425 & 429 have been preserved by the Belfast and County Down Railway.

428 has been preserved by Westrail.

430 was broken up for spares for 428.

▲ **Worksplate of NIR 101 Class locomotive no. 101.**

Neil Webster

501 CLASS (F)   0–4–0 + 0–4–0

Built: 1954 by Walker Brothers, Wigan.
Engine: Two Gardner of 224 hp (267 kW) each.
Transmission: Mechanical.
Transmission Type:
Max. Tractive Effort: 10300 lbf (46 kN).
Cont. Tractive Effort:
Power At Rail:
Weight: 23 tons.
Length Over Buffers:
Wheel Diameter: 2 ft 3 in (686 mm).
Maximum Speed:
Works Numbers: D31–33 in order.
Gauge: 3 ft 0 in.

Loco No.	Date to Traffic	Date Stopped	Date Withdrawn	Month Cut	Cut Up/Store Location
501	24.10.55	31.01.61	31.01.61	.68	Inchicore Works.
502	24.10.55	31.01.61	31.01.61	.68	Inchicore Works.
503	24.10.55	31.01.61	31.01.61	.68	Inchicore Works.

These locomotives were numbered 500–502 until 1957 when they were renumbered in order to 501–503. They were constructed for use on the West Clare Railway (narrow gauge) and were withdrawn when the railway closed.

601 CLASS(G)   B

Built: 1956–57 by Motorenfabrik Deutz at Köln, West Germany.
Engine: Deutz V8 of 130 hp (97 kW).
Transmission: Hydraulic.
Transmission Type: Voith Chain Drive.
Max. Tractive Effort:
Cont. Tractive Effort:
Power At Rail:
Weight: 18 tons.
Length Over Buffers: 20 ft 8 in (6.3 m).
Wheel Diameter: 3 ft 1½ in (950 mm).
Maximum Speed: 20 mph.
Works Numbers: 56118–56120 in order.
Not equipped with train brakes.

Loco No.	Date to Traffic	Date Stopped	Date Withdrawn	Month Cut	Cut Up/Store Location
601	01.06.56	22.07.72	27.04.78		Inchicore Works (P).
602	02.01.57	05.05.65	27.04.78	07.81	Inchicore Works.
603	11.03.57	07.10.69	27.04.78	07.81	Inchicore Works.

601 has been preserved privately.

611 CLASS (G)   B

Built: 1961–62 by Motorenfabrik Deutz at Köln, West Germany.
Engine: Deutz V8 of 160 hp (119 kW).
Transmission: Hydraulic.
Transmission Type: Voith Chain Drive.
Max. Tractive Effort:
Cont. Tractive Effort:
Power At Rail:
Weight: 22 tons.
Length Over Buffers: 21 ft 2 in (6.45 m).
Wheel Diameter: 3 ft 1½ in (950 mm).
Maximum Speed: 20 mph.
Works Numbers: 57225–57231 in order.

Loco No.	Date to Traffic	Date Stopped	Date Withdrawn	Month Cut	Cut Up/Store Location
611	01.06.62	01.02.77	29.09.77		Limerick Wagon Works (P).
612	25.05.62	19.07.71	25.02.77	07.81	Inchicore Works
613	05.06.62	17.01.77	29.09.77		Downpatrick (P).
614	08.06.62	12.12.67	25.02.77	07.81	Inchicore Works.
615	05.06.62	11.01.77	29.09.77	05.89	Thurles Sugar Factory.
616	04.06.62	02.05.77	29.09.77		Mallow (P).
617	24.05.62	09.12.76	14.11.77		Mallow (P).

Locomotives 611, 613, 615, 616, 617 were originally sold to Comhlucht Siuicre Eireann (Irish Sugar Company) on 29.09.77 (except 617 14.11.77) for use at their premises at Carlow (616), Thurles (611, 615 & 617) and Tuam (613).

611 was returned to Limerick and "adopted" by CIE for shunting duties in the Wagon Works. This locomotive is now preserved privately.

613 is preserved by Westrail but is currently on loan to the Downpatrick & Ardglass Railway.

615 was heavily cannibalised for 616 & 617 and was finally broken up during 1989 by the GSRPS.

616 later moved to the premises at Thurles and was then preserved along with 617 by the Great Southern Railway Preservation Society for use on the Tralee–Fenit line.

801 CLASS (K)   0–8–0

Built: 1954 by Maschinenbau Kiel, Kiel, West Germany, for GNR (I).
Engine: MAK of 800 hp (597 kW).
Transmission: Hydraulic.
Transmission Type: Voith Torque Converter.
Max. Tractive Effort: 25100 lbf (112 kN).
Cont. Tractive Effort: 5760 lbf (26 kN) at 37 mph.
Power At Rail:
Weight: 56.75 tons.
Length Over Buffers: 37 ft 2 in (11.33 m).
Wheel Diameter: 4 ft 1¼ in (1250 mm).
Maximum Speed: 50 mph.
Works Number: 800028.

Loco No.	Date to Traffic	Date Stopped	Date Reinstated	Date Stopped	Date Withdrawn	Location
801	.12.54	07.09.67	01.10.74	01.11.74	17.10.76	Galway Metal Co., Galway.

This locomotive was formerly used as a stationary generator but has now been partially cut up. Some remains of this locomotive were still extant at the time of publication, being visible on the up side of the line at 121 miles 32 chains.

▲ Unique K class no. 801 sporting faded green livery at Inchicore in 1964.

Herbert Richards

▼ CIE/Park Royal built Open Standard 1409 stabled at Dublin Connolly on 20th July 1987.

Robert Greengrass

COACHING STOCK

NOTES ON COACHING STOCK

The coaching stock fleet of Irish Rail has recently undergone a programme of renewal and rationalisation. Several of the Park Royal vehicles have recently been refurbished internally whilst the delivery of Mark 3 loco-hauled and push/pull driving and intermediate vehicles has now been completed. Dublin Suburban services , which up to 1984 were almost entirely operated by 201 Class locomotives on push/pull sets made up from converted AEC railcars, are now in the hands of the DART electric multiple units for the Inner Suburban area, with the few remaining Outer Suburban area trains being worked either by locomotives and coaches, mark 3 push/pull sets with modified 121 Class locomotives or NIR 80 Class multiple units currently on lease to Irish Rail.

All steam heated vehicles operate with a boiler van in the train formation and all electrically heated vehicles operate with a generator van in the train formation as no IR locomotives are capable of supplying any form of train heating. A small diesel generator is provided in the boiler vans to provide power for the train lighting system, eliminating the need for each vehicle to carry a dynamo, alternator or batteries. The generator set in generator vans also supplies all auxiliary equipment on electrically heated vehicles.

STOCK LIST

Note: All vehicles are of Open configuration unless otherwise stated.

CIE/PARK ROYAL   STANDARD

Built: 1955 by CIE at Inchicore Works, Dublin, from parts supplied by Park Royal Vehicles, London.
Seats: 82 (*79, §81, †76).   **Heating System:** Steam.
Brakes: Vacuum.   **Bogies:** Commonwealth.
Weight: 26 tons.   **Length:** 61 ft 6 in (18.75 m).
Width: 10 ft 2 in (3.1 m).
r—refurbished.

1379	1389	1399*	1405	1413*
1383	1390	1400r	1406	1415r*
1384r*	1391	1401	1407r	1416
1385*	1394r†	1402r*	1409§	1417r*
1386§	1395r*	1403r	1410r	1418
1387	1396§	1404	1411	1419
1388r*	1398*			

CIE/PARK ROYAL   STANDARD

Built: 1956 by CIE at Inchicore Works, Dublin, from parts supplied by Park Royal Vehicles, London.
Seats: 82 (*79).   **Heating System:** Steam.
Brakes: Vacuum   **Bogies:** Commonwealth.
Weight: 27¼ tons.   **Length:** 61 ft 6 in (18.75 m).
Width: 10 ft 2 in (3.1 m).

1420r*	1422	1425r	1426	1428

CIE/CRAVENS   STANDARD

Built: 1963 by CIE at Inchicore Works, Dublin, from bodyshells and parts supplied by Cravens Ltd., Sheffield.
Seats: 64.   **Heating System:** Steam.
Brakes: Vacuum.   **Bogies:** B4.
Weight: 28.7 tons.   **Length:** 62 ft 8 in (19.1m).
Width: 9 ft 6 in (2.9m).

1504	1506	1508	1510	1513
1505	1507	1509	1511	

CIE/CRAVENS   STANDARD

Built: 1964 by CIE at Inchicore Works, Dublin, from bodyshells and parts supplied by Cravens Ltd., Sheffield.
Seats: 64 (*44).
Brakes: Vacuum.
Weight: 28.7 tons.
Width: 9 ft 6 in (2.9m).

Heating System: Steam.
Bogies: B4. (§ Milden Deutz).
Length: 62 ft 8 in (19.1m).

* Fitted with Bar.

1514	1520*	1525	1531	1539
1515	1521	1526	1532	1540
1516	1522	1528	1533	1541
1517	1523	1529	1535	1542
1518*	1524	1530	1536	1543§
1519				

CIE/CRAVENS   STANDARD

Built: 1967 by CIE at Inchicore Works, Dublin, from bodyshells and parts supplied by Cravens Ltd., Sheffield.
Seats: 64.
Brakes: Vacuum.
Weight: 28.7 tons.
Width: 9 ft 6 in (2.9m).

Heating System: Steam.
Bogies: B4.
Length: 62 ft 8 in (19.1m).

1544	1547	1550	1554	1557
1545	1548	1551	1555	1558
1546	1549	1552	1556	

CIE/PARK ROYAL   BRAKE STANDARD

Built: 1955 by CIE at Inchicore Works, Dublin, from parts supplied by Park Royal Vehicles, London.
Seats: 60 (*76).
Brakes: Vacuum.
Weight: 27.5 tons.
Width: 10 ft 2 in (3.1m).

Heating System: Steam.
Bogies: Commonwealth.
Length: 61 ft 6 in (18.75m).

1941*	1943	1945	1947	1948
1942*	1944	1946		

CIE   TRAVELLING POST OFFICE

Built: 1958 by CIE at Inchicore Works, Dublin.
Seats: Nil.
Brakes: Vacuum & air through piped.
Weight: 29 tons.
Width: 9 ft 6 in (2.9m).

Heating System: Steam.
Bogies: Commonwealth.
Length: 61 ft 6 in (18.75m).

2973	2975	2976	2977	2978
2974				

▲ CIE built Travelling Post Office Van 2976 stabled at Cork, September 1989.

Andrew Marshall

▼ Dundalk Engineering/Werkspoor built Brake Generating steam van 3157. Note the typically Dutch slab sided design of these vehicles.

Andrew Marshall

GSR/CIE   TRAVELLING POST OFFICE

Built: 1935–36 by GSR at Inchicore Works, Dublin.
Rebuilt: 1968 by CIE at Inchicore Works, Dublin.
Seats: Nil.   **Heating System:** Steam.
Brakes: Vacuum & air through piped.   **Bogies:** GSR Design.
Weight: 29 tons.   **Length:** 60 ft (18.29m).
Width: 9 ft (2.74m).

These vehicles were converted in 1968 from earlier passenger vehicles.

2979	2980	2981

DUNDALK ENGINEERING/WERKSPOOR
BRAKE GENERATING STEAM VAN

Built: 1969 by Dundalk Engineering Works, Dundalk, from parts supplied by Werkspoor, Utrecht, Netherlands.
Seats: Nil.   **Bogies:** Werkspoor Design.
Brakes: Vacuum.   **Length:** 44 ft 3 in (13.49m).
Weight: 32 tons.   **Boilers:** Two Spanner of 1000 lb/hr.
Width: 9 ft (2.74m).
Generator: Lister HR3 of 32¼ bhp at 1500 rpm.

3157	3159	3161	3163	3165
3158	3160	3162	3164	3166

VARIOUS/BREL   BRAKE GENERATING STEAM VAN

Built: 1952–56 by BR (Charles Roberts§, Gloucester RCW*)
Rebuilt: 1972 by BREL at Derby Litchurch Lane Works.
Seats: Nil.   **Bogies:** B5.
Brakes: Vacuum.   **Length:** 63ft 5 in (19.33m).
Weight: 37.18 tons.   **Boiler:** Spanner of 2000 lb/hr.
Width: 9 ft (2.74m).
Generator: Lister HR3 of 32¼ hp at 1500 rpm.

These vehicles were converted in 1972 from earlier BR Mark 1 BSKs or BCKs (former numbers in parentheses).

w Also fitted with through air pipe.

3171 (21140§)	3176 (21137§)	3182 (34685)	3187w (34012)
3172 (21138§)	3177 (34227)	3183w (34687)	3188w (34701)
3173 (21146§)	3178w (34590*)	3184 (34566)	3189w (34264)
3174 (21143§)	3179w (34677)	3185 (34093)	3190w (34262)
3175 (21196§)	3180w (34378)	3186w (34757)	3192w (34565)

BREL/CIE   STANDARD

Built: 1972 by BREL at Derby Litchurch Lane Works to Mark 2D design with final minor finishing work by CIE at Inchicore Works, Dublin.
Seats: 56 (§62).   **Heating System:** Air Conditioning.
Brakes: Vacuum.   **Bogies:** B4.
Weight: 32 tons.   **Length:** 66 ft (20.12m).
Width: 9 ft (2.74m).

5101	5102	5103§	5104	5105§

BREL/CIE   FIRST

Built: 1972 by BREL at Derby Litchurch Lane Works to Mark 2D design with final minor finishing work by CIE at Inchicore Works, Dublin.
Seats: 42.   **Heating System:** Air Conditioning.
Brakes: Vacuum.   **Bogies:** B4.
Weight: 32 tons.   **Length:** 66 ft (20.12m).
Width: 9 ft (2.74m).

5106

BREL/CIE   STANDARD

Built: 1972 by BREL at Derby Litchurch Lane Works to Mark 2D design with final minor finishing work by CIE at Inchicore Works, Dublin.
Seats: 54.   **Heating System:** Air Conditioning.
Brakes: Vacuum.   **Bogies:** B4.
Weight: 31.96 tons.   **Length:** 66 ft (20.12m).
Width: 9 ft (2.74m).

This vehicle is fitted with centre doors as it was originally a composite.

5151

BREL/CIE   COMPOSITE

Built: 1972 by BREL at Derby Litchurch Lane Works to Mark 2D design with final minor finishing work by CIE at Inchicore Works, Dublin.
Seats: 24F, 24S.   **Heating System:** Air Conditioning.
Brakes: Vacuum.   **Bogies:** B4.
Weight: 31.9 tons.   **Length:** 66 ft (20.12m).
Width: 9 ft (2.74m).

5152   5153

BREL/CIE   STANDARD

Built: 1972 by BREL at Derby Litchurch Lane Works to Mark 2D design with final minor finishing work by CIE at Inchicore Works, Dublin.
Seats: 54.   **Heating System:** Air Conditioning.
Brakes: Vacuum.   **Bogies:** B4.
Weight: 31.96 tons.   **Length:** 66 ft (20.12m).
Width: 9 ft (2.74m).

This vehicle is fitted with centre doors as it was originally a composite.

5154

BREL/CIE   COMPOSITE

Built: 1972 by BREL at Derby Litchurch Lane Works to Mark 2D design with final minor finishing work by CIE at Inchicore Works, Dublin.
Seats: 24F, 24S.   **Heating System:** Air Conditioning.
Brakes: Vacuum.   **Bogies:** B4.
Weight: 31.9 tons.   **Length:** 66 ft (20.12m).
Width: 9 ft (2.74m).

5155

BREL/CIE STANDARD

Built: 1972 by BREL at Derby Litchurch Lane Works to Mark 2D design with final minor finishing work by CIE at Inchicore Works, Dublin.

Seats: 54.
Brakes: Vacuum.
Weight: 31.96 tons.
Width: 9 ft (2.74m).

Heating System: Air Conditioning.
Bogies: B4.
Length: 66 ft (20.12m).

These vehicles are fitted with centre doors as they were designed to be composites.

5156	5157	5158	5159

BREL/CIE STANDARD

Built: 1972 by BREL at Derby Litchurch Lane Works to Mark 2D design with final minor finishing work by CIE at Inchicore Works, Dublin.

Seats: 64.
Brakes: Vacuum.
Weight: 30.96 tons.
Width: 9 ft (2.74m).

Heating System: Air Conditioning.
Bogies: B4.
Length: 66 ft (20.12m).

5201	5209	5216	5223	5230
5202	5210	5217	5224	5231
5203	5211	5218	5225	5232
5204	5212	5219	5226	5233
5205	5213	5220	5227	5234
5206	5214	5221	5228	5235
5207	5215	5222	5229	5236
5208				

▲ **BREL/CIE built Mark 2D Open Standard no. 5214 sporting the current IR Inter City livery.**
Andrew Marshall

27

BREL/CIE   RESTAURANT BUFFET STANDARD

Built: 1972 by BREL at Derby Litchurch Lane Works to Mark 2D design with final minor finishing work by CIE at Inchicore Works, Dublin.

Seats: 30 (*36).   **Heating System:** Air Conditioning.
Brakes: Vacuum.   **Bogies:** B4.
Weight: 34.2 tons.   **Length:** 66 ft (20.12m).
Width: 9 ft (2.74m).

5401	5403	5405	5406	5407
5402	5404*			

BREL/CIE   PRESIDENTIAL COACH

Built: 1972 by BREL at Derby Litchurch Lane Works to Mark 2D design with final minor finishing work by CIE at Inchicore Works, Dublin.
Rebuilt: 1977 by CIE at Inchicore Works, Dublin.

Seats: Loose chairs as required.   **Heating System:** Air Conditioning.
Brakes: Vacuum.   **Bogies:** B4.
Weight: 34.2 tons.   **Length:** 66 ft (20.12m).
Width: 9 ft (2.74m).

This vehicle is used to convey the President of Ireland and other VIPs on special occasions

5408

BREL/CIE   RESTAURANT BUFFET STANDARD

Built: 1972 BREL at Derby Litchurch Lane Works to Mark 2D design, with minor finishing work completed by CIE at Inchicore Works, Dublin.

Seats: 30.   **Heating System:** Air Conditioning.
Brakes: Vacuum.   **Bogies:** B4.
Weight: 34.2 tons.   **Length:** 66 ft (20.12m).
Width: 9 ft (2.74m).

5410	5411

Vehicle 5409 was severely damaged by a fire bomb during 1985 and has been withdrawn. This vehicle is stored at Inchicore Works awaiting disposal.

BREL/CIE   BRAKE GENERATOR VAN

Built: 1972 BREL at Derby Litchurch Lane Works to Mark 2D, design with minor finishing work completed by CIE at Inchicore Works, Dublin.

Seats: Nil.   **Heating System:** Electric through wired.
Brakes: Vacuum.   **Bogies:** B5.
Weight: 39.95 tons.   **Length:** 66 ft (20.12m).
Width: 9 ft (2.74m)
Engines: Two Detroit 8V–71N (Model No. 7083–7005) of 234 hp at 1575 rpm.
Alternators: Two International Electric of 160 kW.

5601	5603	5605	5607	5609
5602	5604	5606	5608	5610

IR   DRIVING BRAKE GENERATOR STANDARD

Built: 1988–89 by IR at Inchicore Works, Dublin to BREL Mark 3 design & fitted with automatic plug type doors.

Seats: 55 (plus 6 tip up).   **Heating:** Pressure Ventilated.
Brakes: Air.   **Bogies:** Linke Hoffman Busch. (* BT22C)
Weight: 41 tons.   **Length:** 22.70 m.
Width: 9 ft (2.74m).   **Alternator:** Reliance.
Engine: Cummins NTA855R1 of 310 hp (231 kW) at 1500 rpm.

These vehicles can only operate in conjunction with 6301–6319 series vehicles and modified 121 Class locomotives.

6101	6102	6103	6104*	6105*

IR   INTERMEDIATE STANDARD

Built: 1988–89 by IR at Inchicore Works, Dublin to BREL Mark 3 design & fitted with automatic plug type doors.

Seats: 76.   **Heating System:** Pressure Ventilated.
Brakes: Air.   **Bogies:** BT22.
Weight: 34 tons.   **Length:** 74 ft (22.57m).
Width: 9 ft (2.74m).

These vehicles can only operate in conjunction with 6101–6105 series vehicles and modified 121 Class locomotives.

6301	6305	6309	6313	6317
6302	6306	6310	6314	6318
6303	6307	6311	6315	6319
6304	6308	6312	6316	

BREL/CIE/IR   STANDARD (§FIRST)

Built: (7101–44) 1984–86 by BREL at Derby Litchurch Lane Works, with minor finishing work completed by CIE at Inchicore Works, Dublin. (7145–7160) 1986–87 by CIE/IR at Inchicore Works, Dublin. All to BREL Mark 3 design & fitted with automatic plug–type doors.

Seats: 72S (§64F)(*66S).   **Heating System:** Air Conditioning.
Brakes: Air.   **Bogies:** BT22.
Weight: 35 tons.   **Length:** 74 ft (22.57m).
Width: 9 ft (2.74m).

7101	7113	7125	7137	7149
7102	7114	7126	7138	7150
7103	7115	7127	7139	7151
7104	7116	7128	7140	7152
7105	7117	7129	7141	7153
7106	7118	7130	7142	7154
7107§	7119	7131	7143	7155
7108	7120	7132	7144	7156
7109	7121	7133	7145	7157§
7110	7122	7134	7146	7158
7111	7123	7135	7147*	7159
7112	7124	7136	7148	7160

CIE/IR   EXECUTIVE COACH

Built: 1987 by CIE/IR at Inchicore Works, Dublin, to BREL Mark 3 design & fitted with automatic plug type doors.

Seats: Variable as required.   **Heating System:** Air Conditioning.
Brakes: Air.   **Bogies:** BT22.
Weight: 35 tons.   **Length:** 74 ft (22.57m).
Width: 9 ft (2.74m).

§ Fitted with cocktail bar.

7161§	7162

CIE/IR STANDARD

Built: 1987 by CIE/IR at Inchicore Works, Dublin, to BREL Mark 3 design & fitted with automatic plug type doors.
Seats: 72.
Brakes: Air.
Weight: 35 tons.
Width: 9 ft (2.74m).
Heating System: Air Conditioning.
Bogies: BT22.
Length: 74 ft (22.57m).

7163	7164

CIE/IR COMPOSITE

Built: 1987–88 by CIE/IR at Inchicore Works, Dublin, to BREL Mark 3 design & fitted with automatic plug type doors.
Seats: 16F, 52S.
Brakes: Air.
Weight: 35 tons.
Width: 9 ft (2.74m).
Heating System: Air Conditioning.
Bogies: BT22.
Length: 74 ft (22.57m).

7165	7167	7169	7171	7172
7166	7168	7170		

BREL/CIE/IR RESTAURANT BUFFET STANDARD

Built: (7401–5) 1984–86 by BREL at Derby Litchurch Lane Works, with minor finishing work by CIE at Inchicore Works, Dublin. (7406–13) 1986–88 by CIE/IR at Inchicore Works, Dublin. All to BREL Mark 3 design & fitted with automatic plug–type doors.
Seats: 30 (*31).
Brakes: Air.
Weight: 37.2 tons.
Width: 9 ft (2.74m).
Heating System: Air Conditioning.
Bogies: BT22B.
Length: 74 ft (22.57m).

7401*	7404	7407	7410	7412
7402	7405	7408	7411	7413
7403	7406	7409		

BREL/CIE/IR BRAKE GENERATOR VAN

Built: (7601–7) 1984–86 by BREL at Derby Litchurch Lane Works, with minor finishing work completed by CIE at Inchicore Works, Dublin. (7608–15) 1986–88 by CIE/IR at Inchicore Works, Dublin. All to BREL Mark 3 design.
Seats: Nil.
Brakes: Air.
Weight: 35.8 tons.
Width: 9 ft (2.74m).
Heatign System: Electric through wired.
Bogies: BT22C.
Length: 74 ft (22.57m).
Engines: Two Detroit 8V–71N (Model No. 7083–7201) of 234 hp (174 kW) at 1575 rpm (* Two Cummins of 295 hp (220 kW).)
Alternators: Two Newton Derby of 168 kW.

7601	7604	7607	7610*	7613*
7602	7605	7608*	7611*	7614*
7603	7606	7609*	7612*	7615*

ELECTRIC MULTIPLE UNITS

Depot: Dublin Fairview.

LINKE–HOFMANN BUSCH   DART TWO CAR UNITS

Built: 1983 by Linke–Hofmann Busch at Salzgitter, West Germany.
Seats: 72S per car (* plus 16 tip–up), open seating layout.
Brakes: Rheostatic/Regenerative (1st Service brake). Air/Load Dependent (2nd Service Brake).
Wheel Diameter: 2 ft 9½ in (840mm).   **Width:** 9 ft 6 in (2.9m).
Length: 67 ft 2.7 in (20.49m).   **Maximum Speed:** 62½ mph (100 kph).

DRIVING MOTOR STANDARD

Weight: 40.34 tons.
System: 1500v dc overhead.
Traction Motors: Four GEC of 174hp (130kW).

8101*	8109	8117*	8125*	8133
8102	8110*	8118*	8126	8134
8103*	8111*	8119	8127*	8135
8104	8112	8120	8128*	8136
8105*	8113*	8121	8129	8137*
8106	8114*	8122*	8130*	8138
8107*	8115	8123*	8131*	8139*
8108	8116	8124*	8132	8140

DRIVING TRAILER STANDARD

Weight: 25.43 tons.

8301*	8309	8317*	8325*	8333
8302	8310*	8318*	8326	8334
8303*	8311*	8319	8327*	8335
8304	8312	8320	8328*	8336
8305*	8313*	8321	8329	8337*
8306	8314*	8322*	8330*	8338
8307*	8315	8323*	8331*	8339*
8308	8316	8324*	8332	8340

Each two car unit comprises a DMSO and a DTSO which are semi permanently coupled. It is usual for the last two digits of the number of each car to be the same i.e. two car set comprising 8101+8301.

Maximum service combination is three units, which can be coupled by means of the fully automatic Scharfenberg coupler.

Tip up seats are being removed from each unit as they pass through Works.

SECTION 2–NORTHERN IRELAND RAILWAYS STOCK LIST.

BRIEF HISTORY

Until nationalisation on 1st January 1948 railway services in Northern Ireland were operated by two main constituent companies, The Northern Counties Committee (NCC) and The Belfast & County Down Railway. (B & CDR). The new nationalised concern was known as the Ulster Transport Authority (UTA). In 1958 the lines of the previously independent GNR(I) in Northern Ireland were absorbed when this company was divided between the UTA and CIE The railways of the UTA passed to Northern Ireland Railways with effect from 1st April 1968 when the former concern was dissolved.

LOCOMOTIVE CLASSIFICATION

NIR diesel locomotives are identified by a two letter code by the operating department. These codes are shown in brackets in the class headings.

LOCOMOTIVES

1 CLASS (DH)   0–6–0

Built: 1969 by English Electric at Vulcan Foundry, Newton Le Willows.
Engine: Dorman 12QTV of 620 hp (463 kW) at 1800 rpm.
Transmission: Hydraulic.
Transmission Type: EE Twin Disc DBSG138–2 Torque Converter coupled to a Wiseman 15RLGB Final Frive.
Max. Tractive Effort: 25000 lbf (111 kN).
Cont. Tractive Effort:
Power At Rail:
Weight: 42.5 tons.
Length Over Buffers: 28 ft 4 in (8.64m).
Wheel Diameter: 3 ft 6 in (1067 mm).
Maximum Speed: 29 mph.
Works Numbers: D1266–D1268 in order.

Loco No.	Date to Traffic	Date Stopped	Date Withdrawn	Cut Up/Store Location
1	31.07.69	. .86	.05.89	Lisburn (P)
2	27.09.69	09.09.89	09.09.89	Belfast York Road
3	04.10.69	. .88	.05.89	Belfast York Road

No.1 is preserved as a static exhibit by the NIR.

No.2 was originally withdrawn in May 1989, but was specially reinstated and repainted for a farewell railtour on 10.09.89. However, the locomotive then suffered a major engine failure on 09.09.89 which resulted in its final withdrawal.

101 CLASS (DL)   Bo–Bo

Built: 1970 by B.R.E.L. at Doncaster, as sub–contactors for The Hunslet Engine Company, Leeds.
Engine: English Electric 8CSVT of 1350hp (1007 kW) at 850 rpm.
Transmission: Electric.
Traction Motors: English Electric 253AZ.
Max. Tractive Effort: 42000 lbf (187 kN).
Cont. Tractive Effort: 25200 lbf (112 kN) at 15 mph.

Power At Rail:
Weight: 68 tons.
Length Over Buffers: 45 ft 2 in (13.77m).
Wheel Diameter: 3 ft 4 in (1016 mm).
Maximum Speed: 80 mph.
Works Numbers: Hunslet 7197–7199 in order.

Loco No.	Fittings	Date to Traffic	Name
101	OAER	04.07.70	EAGLE
102	OAER	04.07.70	FALCON
103	OAER	04.07.70	MERLIN

104 CLASS (MV)   Bo–Bo

Built: 1956–57 by Metropolitan Vickers at Dukinfield Works, Manchester.
Original Engine: Crossley ESTV8 of 550 hp (410 kW).
Rebuilt: 1970–79 by CIE at Inchicore Works, Dublin.
Current Engine: General Motors 8–B645E of 1100 hp (821 kW) at 900 rpm.
Transmission: Electric.
Traction Motors: Metropolitan Vickers MV137CW.
Max. Tractive Effort: 34440 lbf (153 kN).
Cont. Tractive Effort:
Power At Rail: 842 hp (629 kW).
Weight: 61.5 tons.
Length Over Buffers: 42 ft (12.80 m).
Wheel Diameter: 3 ft 2 in (965 mm).
Maximum Speed: 80 mph.
Works Numbers: 962, 964, 973, 974, 976, 980 in order. All works plates show built 1956.

For further details see Irish Rail 201 Class.

Loco No.	Fittings	Date to Traffic	Former CIE Number
104	NR	23.02.86	216
105	N		218
106	NR	23.06.86	227
107	NR	10.09.86	228
108	NR	03.12.87	230
109	NR	25.03.86	234

Work on the conversion of 218 to 105 had not yet commenced at the date of publication.

It was originally intended that 224 would become 105, but this loco was rejected by the NIR upon delivery to York Road Works, Belfast. This locomotive remains at York Road as a source of spares for the remaining locomotives.

CAWS fittings on locomotives 224/7/30/4 were removed by CIE before sale.

▲ **Nameplate of 80 class power car no. 81.**

Neil Webster

111 CLASS (GM)   Co–Co

Built: 1980–84 by General Motors, La Grange, Illinois, U.S.A.
Engine: General Motors 12–645E3B of 2475 hp (1845 kW) at 900 rpm.
Transmission: Electric.
Traction Motors: General Motors D77B.
Max. Tractive Effort: 55100 lbf (245 kN).
Cont. Tractive Effort: 46850 lbf (209 kN) at 15.1 mph.
Power At Rail: 1823 hp (1360 kW).
Weight: 99 tons.
Length Over Buffers: 57 ft (17.37 m).
Wheel Diameter: 3 ft 4 in (1016 mm).
Maximum Speed: 90 mph.
Works Numbers: 798072/1, 798072/2, 838084 in order.
Multiple Working: Within class & with IR classes 071, 121, 141 & 181.

Loco No.	Fittings	Date to Traffic	Name
111	SAMR	03.02.81	GREAT NORTHERN
112	SAMR	03.02.81	NORTHERN COUNTIES
113	SAMR	07.08.84	BELFAST & Co DOWN

DIESEL ELECTRIC MULTIPLE UNITS (CURRENT CLASSES)

80 CLASS

DRIVING MOTOR BRAKE STANDARD

Built: 1974–78 BREL at Derby Litchurch Lane Works.
Engine: English Electric 4SRKT turbo–charged of 560 hp (418 kW) at 850 rpm.
Traction Motors: Two EE 538 of 220 hp (164 kW) mounted on the power car bogie remote from the engine.

Seats: 45 (*35)	**Length:** 65 ft 8 in (20.02 m).	
Width: 9 ft (2.74 m).	**Weight:** 62 tons.	
Bogies: B6.		

Vehicle No.	Sector	Date to Traffic	Month Withdrawn	Month Disposal	Cut Up/Store Location
67	S	22.12.77			
68	-	18.02.78			
69	-	24.01.78			
81	S	26.11.74			
82	S	03.12.74			
83	S	07.01.75			
84	S	24.01.75			
85	S	12.02.75			
86	-	28.02.75			
87	S	25.03.75			
88		14.04.75	03.83	10.88	McConnell Metals, Belfast.
89	S	05.10.75			
90	S	03.02.78			
91	S	21.02.78			
92	S	27.02.78			
93	S	14.04.78			
94	I	19.04.78			
95	I	14.04.78			
96*	I	15.05.78			
97	I	16.06.78			
98*	I	05.07.78			
99	I	06.07.78			

Names

81 THE BOYS BRIGADE	97 GLENSHESK§
94 GLENARIFF	98 GLENOE
95 GLENDUN§	99 SIR MYLES HUMPHREYS
96 GLENSHANE	

§ names allocated but not yet carried.

68, 69 & 86 are currently leased to Irish Rail for use on Dublin Outer Suburban services.

88 was withdrawn following a collision at Hilden on 25.03.83.

DRIVING TRAILER STANDARD

Built: 1974–78 by BREL at Derby Litchurch Lane Works.
Seats: 81.   **Length:** 66 ft (20.12 m).
Width: 9 ft (2.74 m).   **Weight:** 28 tons.
Bogies: B4.

Vehicle No.	Sector	Date to Traffic	Month Withdrawn	Month Disposal	Cut Up/Store Location
731		.10.74	03.82	?	?
732	S	26.11.74			
733	S	05.10.74			
734	S	28.02.75			
735	-	07.01.75			
736	S	24.01.75			
737	-	29.01.75			
738	S	14.04.75			
739	S	25.03.75			
740	-	23.12.77			
741		.01.78	09.79	?	Magheramorne.
742	S	24.01.78			
743	S	18.02.78			
744	S	22.02.78			
745	S	21.02.78			
746	S	14.04.78			
747	I	14.04.78			
748		.05.78	05.79	?	?
749	I	.05.78			
750	I	15.05.78	07.88	-	Belfast York Road.
751	I	16.06.78			

735, 737 & 740 are currently leased to Irish Rail for use on Dublin Outer Suburban services.

731 was withdrawn following a fire bomb incident at Coleraine on 21.03.82.

741 was withdrawn following a bomb incident at Balmoral on 19.09.79. The cab of this vehicle still remains in the undergrowth on the down side of the line at Magheramorne.

748 was withdrawn following a fire at Crumlin on 25.05.79.

750 was withdrawn following a fire at Coleraine on 15.07.88.

DRIVING TRAILER STANDARD

Built: 1969–70 by BREL at Derby Litchurch Lane Works to Mark 2C design.
Seats: 62 (*75).   **Length:** 66 ft (20.12 m).
Width: 9 ft (2.74 m).   **Weight:** 32.5 tons.
Bogies: B4.

These vehicles were formerly BR TSOs 5516 & 5498 respectively.

Vehicle No.	Sector	Date to Traffic
752*	I	.81
753	I	05.84

▲ 80 Class Driving Trailer Open Standard no. 733 at Belfast Central, October 1989.

Neil Webster

▼ 80 Class Trailer Open Standard no. 765 at Antrim, October 1989.

Neil Webster

DRIVING TRAILER BRAKE STANDARD

Built: 1969 by BREL at Derby Litchurch Lane Works to Mark 2B design.
Seats: 31.
Width: 9 ft (2.74 m).
Bogies: B4.
Length: 66 ft (20.12 m).
Weight: 32 tons.

This vehicle was formerly DBSO 811.

Vehicle No.	Sector	Date to Traffic
754	I	.88

TRAILER STANDARD

Built: 1969–74 by BREL at Derby Litchurch Lane Works.
Seats: 87 (*§ 62).
Width: 9 ft (2.74 m).
Bogies: B4.
Length: 66 ft (20.12 m).
Weight: 28 tons (§32 tons, *32.5 tons).

774 was formerly BR Mark 2C TSO 5521.
776, 778, 779 & 780 were formerly TSOs 824, 826, 827 & 828 respectively.

Vehicle No.	Sector	Date to Traffic	Month Withdrawn	Month Disposal	Cut Up/Store Location
761	-	26.11.74			
762	S	03.12.74			
763	S	05.10.74			
764	S	07.01.75			
765	S	18.07.77			
766	S	08.08.77			
767	-	01.08.77			
768	S	24.01.78			
769	S	23.11.77			
770		11.77	09.79	?	?
771	S	11.11.77			
772	-	18.02.78			
773	I	21.02.78			
774§	I	.81			
776*	I	12.06.84			
778§	I	12.01.84			
779§	I	11.07.84			
780§	I	23.03.84			

761, 767 & 772 are currently leased to Irish Rail for Dublin Outer Suburban services.

770 was withdrawn following a bomb incident at Balmoral on 19.09.79.

CASTLE CLASS

DRIVING MOTOR BRAKE STANDARD

Built: 1985–87 by BREL at Derby Litchurch Lane Works.
Engine: English Electric 4SRKT turbo–charged of 550 (*560) hp (410 kW or *417 kW) at 850 rpm.
Traction Motors: Two EE 538 of 220 hp (164 kW) mounted on the power car bogie remote from the engine.
Seats: 38 (plus 13 tip–up).
Width: 9 ft (2.74 m).
Bogies: BR Mk.6.
Length: 65 ft 8 in (20.02 m).
Weight: 62 tons.

The power equipment used on these units was salvaged from the former 70 class units, except for 457 whose power equipment was salvaged from 80 class vehicle 88.

Vehicle No.	Sector	Date to Traffic
451	S	28.10.85
452	S	09.11.85
453	S	25.02.86
454	S	06.03.86
455	S	.05.86
456	S	.07.86
457*	S	.11.86
458	S	21.01.87
459	S	05.06.87

Names

451 BELFAST CASTLE
452 OLDERFLEET CASTLE
453 MOIRY CASTLE
454 CARRICKFERGUS CASTLE
455 GALGORM CASTLE
456 GOSFORD CASTLE
457 BANGOR CASTLE
458 ANTRIM CASTLE
459 KILLYLEAGH CASTLE

DRIVING TRAILER STANDARD

Built: 1985–87 by BREL at Derby Litchurch Lane Works.
Seats: 68 (plus 15 tip–up).　**Length:** 65 ft 8 in (20.02 m).
Width: 9 ft (2.74 m).　**Weight:** 32.4 tons.
Bogies: B4.

Vehicle No.	Sector	Date to Traffic
781	S	28.10.85
782	S	09.11.85
783	S	25.02.86
784	S	06.03.86
785	S	.05.86
786	S	.07.86
787	S	.11.86
788	S	21.01.87
789	S	05.06.87

TRAILER STANDARD

Seats: 78 (plus 15 tip–up).　**Length:** 66 ft (20.12 m).
Width: 9 ft (2.74 m).　**Weight:** 30.4 tons.
Bogies: B4.

Vehicle No.	Sector	Date to Traffic
791	S	28.10.85
792	S	09.11.85
793	S	25.02.86
794	S	06.03.86
795	S	.05.86
796	S	.07.86
797	S	.11.86
798	S	21.01.87
799	S	05.06.87

LEYLAND RAILBUS

Built: 1981 by BREL at Derby Litchurch Lane Works.
Engine: Leyland 690 of 200 hp (149 kW).
Transmission: Mechanical. SCG type SE4 epicyclic gearbox and cardan shafts to SCG type RF28 final drive.
Seats: 56S.
Width: 8 ft (2.44 m).
Maximum Speed: 75 mph.
Length: 50 ft 2¼ in (15.3 m).
Weight: 19.40 tons.

This manufacturers prototype was used as a demonstrator on British Rail before being sold to the NIR and was formerly BR RDB977020

Vehicle No.	Sector	Date to Traffic
R3	I	?

COACHING STOCK
NOTES ON COACHING STOCK

All NIR coaching stock has been purchased from BREL either new or second hand since 1969 when a major coaching stock renewal programme was approved. This included the introduction of a locomotive hauled "Enterprise Express" train between Belfast and Dublin powered by one of the three new locomotives built by BREL at Doncaster Works as subcontractors for The Hunslet Engine Company, Leeds. An initial order of eight vehicles, followed later by a further order of five vehicles was utilised for this service, all being bought new from BREL. In 1981, following the arrival of the 111 Class locomotives, a further order of 12 vehicles was made, all being second hand ex BR Western Region. This has since been supplemented by the arrival of eight more vehicles, but some of the original order have now been converted to multiple unit vehicles. A programme of rolling stock refurbishment is still under way, with all vehicles now gradually being repainted into their new sector liveries whilst remaining compartment stock is being converted to open plan seating accommodation. Most recent addition to the coaching stock fleet is ex BR Mark 2F 3367, which entered service on 21st January 1989 still carrying it's BR blue & grey livery. Renumbering of the 62 seat vehicles is taking place into the 93x series for ease of identification by the operating department.

STOCK LIST

Note: All passenger coaching stock is of Open layout unless otherwise stated. All vehicles are allocated to the InterCity sector.

BREL   GRILL/BAR/DINING CAR

Built: 1973 by BREL at Derby Litchurch Lane Works to Mark 2F design.
Seats: 24.
Brakes: Air.
Weight: 37 tons.
Width: 9 ft (2.74 m).
Heating System: Air Conditioning.
Bogies: B5.
Length: 66 ft (20.12 m).

This vehicle was built for BR as TSO 5970, being converted to RSS 1800 in 1974 and subsequently purchased by NIR in 1982.

546

BREL   GRILL/BAR/DINING CAR

Built: 1969 by BREL at Derby Litchurch Lane Works to Mark 2B design.
Seats: 22.
Brakes: Air.
Weight: 33 tons.
Width: 9 ft (2.74 m).

Heating System: Pressure Ventilated.
Bogies: B4.
Length: 66 ft (20.12 m).

Push/Pull Fitted.

547

BREL   DRIVING BRAKE STANDARD

Built: 1969 by BREL at Derby Litchurch Lane Works to Mark 2B design.
Seats: 31.
Brakes: Air
Weight: 32 tons.
Width: 9 ft (2.74 m).

Heating System: Pressure Ventilated.
Bogies: B4.
Length: 66 ft (20.12 m).

Push/Pull Fitted.

812

BREL   DRIVING BRAKE FIRST

Built: 1969 by BREL at Derby Litchurch Lane Works to Mark 2C design.

Seats: 24.
Brakes: Air.
Weight: 32 tons.
Width: 9 ft (2.74 m).

Heating System: Pressure Ventilated.
Bogies: B4.
Length: 66 ft (20.12 m).

Push/Pull Fitted.

813

BREL   BUFFET STANDARD

Built: 1969 by BREL at Derby Litchurch Lane Works to Mark 2B design.
Seats: 54.
Brakes: Air.
Weight: 32 tons.
Width: 9 ft (2.74 m).

Heating System: Pressure Ventilated.
Bogies: B4.
Length: 66 ft (20.12 m).

Push/Pull Fitted.

821

BREL   STANDARD

Built: 1969 by BREL at Derby Litchurch Lane Works to Mark 2B design.
Seats: 62.
Brakes: Air.
Weight: 32 tons.
Width: 9 ft (2.74 m).

Heating System: Pressure Ventilated.
Bogies: B4.
Length: 66 ft (20.12 m).

Push/Pull Fitted.
These vehicles are expected to be renumbered to 934 & 935 respectively in the near future.

822   823

▲ BREL built Mark 2F Grill/Bar/Dining Car no. 546 at Belfast Central October 1989.

Neil Webster

▼ BREL built Mark 2B Open Standard no.822. This vehicle is equipped for push/pull working.

Peter Jones

BREL   FIRST

Built: 1969 by BREL at Derby Litchurch Lane Works to Mark 2B design.
Seats: 42.   **Heating System:** Pressure Ventilated.
Brakes: Air.   **Bogies:** B4.
Weight: 32 tons.   **Length:** 66 ft (20.12 m).
Width: 9 ft (2.74 m).

Push/Pull Fitted.
This vehicle was formerly FO 801.

901

BREL   CORRIDOR FIRST

Built: 1969 by BREL at Derby Litchurch Lane Works to Mark 2B design.
Seats: 42.   **Heating System:** Pressure Ventilated.
Brakes: Air.   **Bogies:** B4.
Weight: 33 tons.   **Length:** 66 ft (20.12 m).
Width: 9 ft (2.74 m).

This vehicle was formerly BR FK 13509, being purchased by NIR in 1981. It is expected to be converted to an 80 class TSO (number unknown) in the near future.

902

BREL   FIRST

Built: 1970 by BREL at Derby Litchurch Lane Works to Mark 2C design.
Seats: 42.   **Heating System:** Pressure Ventilated.
Brakes: Air.   **Bogies:** B4.
Weight: 33 tons.   **Length:** 66 ft (20.12 m).
Width: 9 ft (2.74 m).

This vehicle was formerly BR FO 3166, being purchased by NIR in 1983.

903

BREL   FIRST

Built: 1974 by BREL at Derby Litchurch Lane Works to Mark 2F design.
Seats: 42.   **Heating System:** Air Conditioned.
Brakes: Air.   **Bogies:** B4.
Weight: 33.5 tons.   **Length:** 66 ft (20.12 m).
Width: 9 ft (2.74 m).

This vehicle was formerly BR FO 3367, being purchased by NIR in 1988, and retains BR blue/grey livery at the date of publication.

904

BREL   BRAKE STANDARD GENERATOR VAN

Built: 1969 by BREL at Derby Litchurch Lane Works to Mark 2B design. Converted to standard class generator van upon sale to NIR.

Seats: 24.
Brakes: Air.
Weight: 36 tons.
Width: 9 ft (2.74 m).
Engine: Detroit 8V–71N TD2 (Model No. 7083–7005) of 234 hp (175 kW) at 1575 rpm.
Alternator: Markon B range, series 2.

Heating System: Pressure Ventilated.
Bogies: B4/B5.
Length: 66 ft (20.12 m).

This vehicle was formerly BR BFK 14104, being purchased by NIR in 1981. It was converted to open plan seating in 1988.

911

BREL   BRAKE FIRST GENERATOR VAN

Built: 1969 by BREL at Derby Litchurch Lane Works to Mark 2B design. Converted to standard class generator van upon sale to NIR.

Seats: 24.
Brakes: Air.
Weight: 36 tons.
Width: 9 ft (2.74 m).
Engine: Detroit 8V–71N TD2 (Model No. 7083–7005) of 234 hp (175 kW) at 1575 rpm.
Alternator: Markon B range, series 2.

Heating System: Pressure Ventilated.
Bogies: B4/B5.
Length: 66 ft (20.12 m).

This vehicle was formerly BR BFK 14108, being purchased by NIR in 1981. It was converted to first class open plan seating in 1989.

912

BREL   BRAKE EXECUTIVE GENERATOR VAN

Built: 1969 by BREL at Derby Litchurch Lane Works to Mark 2B design. Converted to standard class generator van upon sale to NIR.

Seats: Loose chairs as required.
Brakes: Air.
Weight: 36 tons.
Width: 9 ft (2.74 m).
Engine: Detroit 8V–71N TD2 (Model No. 7083–7005) of 234 hp (175 kW) at 1575 rpm.
Alternator: Markon B range, series 2.

Heating System: Pressure Ventilated.
Bogies: B4/B5.
Length: 66 ft (20.12 m).

This vehicle was formerly BR BFK 14111, being purchased by NIR in 1981. It was converted to an executive vehicle in 1989.

913

BREL   BRAKE STANDARD GENERATOR VAN

Built: 1969 by BREL at Derby Litchurch Lane Works to Mark 2B design. Converted to standard class generator van upon sale to NIR.

Seats: 24.
Brakes: Air.
Weight: 36 tons.
Width: 9 ft (2.74 m).
Engine: Detroit 8V–71N TD2 (Model No. 7083–7005) of 234 hp (175 kW) at 1575 rpm.
Alternator: Markon B range, series 2.

Heating System: Pressure Ventilated.
Bogies: B4/B5.
Length: 66 ft (20.12 m).

These vehicles were formerly BR BFKs 14110 & 14106 respectively, being purchased by NIR 1983. They were converted to open plan seating in 1988 & 1989 respectively.

914   915

▲ BREL built Brake First Generator Van no. 912 sporting the latest NIR InterCity livery.

Neil Webster

▼ BREL built Open standard no. 927 forms part of the 1700 to Dublin Connolly at Belfast Central on 7th October 1989.

Neil Webster

BREL STANDARD (* COMPARTMENT STANDARD)

Built: 1969 by BREL at Derby Litchurch Lane Works to Mark 2B design.
Seats: 52 (*56).
Brakes: Air.
Weight: 33 tons.
Width: 9 ft (2.74 m).

Heating System: Pressure Ventilated.
Bogies: B4.
Length: 66 ft (20.12 m).

921–924 are Push/Pull Fitted.
These vehicles were formerly BR FKs 13490, 13495, 13496, 13508, 13503, 13498, 13506 & 13510 respectively, being purchased by NIR 1981. Converted to open plan seating 1988–89.

921	923	925	927	928*
922*	924	926		

BREL STANDARD

Built: 1969–70 by BREL at Derby Litchurch Lane Works to Mark 2C design.
Seats: 62.
Brakes: Air.
Weight: 32.5 tons.
Width: 9 ft (2.74 m).

Heating System: Pressure Ventilated.
Bogies: B4.
Length: 66 ft (20.12 m).

These vehicles were formerly BR TSOs 5573 & 5531 respectively, being purchased by NIR 1981.

930   931

BREL STANDARD

Built: 1969 by BREL at Derby Litchurch Lane Works to Mark 2C design.
Seats: 62.
Brakes: Air.
Weight: 32.5 tons.
Width: 9 ft (2.74 m).

Heating System: Pressure Ventilated.
Bogies: B4.
Length: 66 ft (20.12 m).

Push/Pull Fitted.
This vehicle was formerly SO 825.

932

BREL STANDARD

Built: 1970 by BREL at Derby Litchurch Lane Works to Mark 2C design.
Seats: 62.
Brakes: Air.
Weight: 32.5 tons.
Width: 9 ft (2.74 m).

Heating System: Pressure Ventilated.
Bogies: B4.
Length: 66 ft (20.12 m).

This vehicle was originally BR TSO 5577, being purchased by NIR 1981, & was previously numbered 929.

933

SECTION 3–LOCOMOTIVE HAULED PASSENGER TRAINS AND BOOKED MOTIVE POWER.

This section is designed to act as firstly, a complete guide to ALL train identification numbers of passenger trains of Irish Rail and Northern Ireland Railways, and secondly, as a complete guide to the booked motive power of all locomotive hauled passenger trains of both railways.

From the information contained in this section it is possible to ascertain the class of locomotive scheduled to work any IR or NIR locomotive hauled passenger train and also details of the previous and subsequent passenger workings (if any) to be performed by the locomotive in question.

First of all the reader should consult the IR or NIR Passenger Timetable for the starting point of the train for which information is required. Then the train should be located in the index of locomotive hauled trains (trains not shown in this index are formed of multiple unit stock) which appears after the locomotive diagrams. The index is arranged in chronological order of departures from the originating station and then as follows:

Heading	- Originating station. (These are in alphabetical order)
1st Column	- Train Identification number.
2nd Column	- Departure time from originating station.
3rd Column	- Days of operation.
4th Column	- Destination station.
5th Column	- Diagram number.

The following abbreviations are used:

M	=	Monday.	S	=	Saturday.
T	=	Tuesday.	SUN	=	Sunday.
W	=	Wednesday.	O	=	Only.
Th	=	Thursday.	X	=	Excepted.
F	=	Friday.	7	=	Daily.

For Example: ThO = Thursdays Only, FX = Fridays Excepted.

P/P	=	Push/Pull Operation.
111	=	Booked NIR Class 111 locomotive.
001	=	Booked IR Class 001 locomotive.
071	=	Booked IR Class 071 locomotive.
121	=	Booked IR Class 121 locomotive.
141	=	Booked IR Class 141 or 181 locomotive.
2x	=	Booked two locomotives of the class shown in multiple.

Once the train required has been located in the index, the diagram number can be consulted in the list of diagrams (arranged in numerical order) for details of the locomotive working. In the diagrams list the information is given in columns as follows, reading from left to right:

Diagram Number: This is the number referred to in the index. The first part of this number refers to the scheduled class of locomotive and the second to the turn number. (e.g. 071.02 denotes booked for a class 071, turn no. 2).

Time: Departure time from the originating station. * Denotes runs only on dates as shown in the Passenger Timetable.

Days of Operation: The symbols used are shown above.

Section of Route: The stations shown are the originating and destination stations of the train in question.

Notes: Other relevant information to the working of the train.

Important Notes.

A) When the booked motive power is shown as a class 141 locomotive, it can also represent a class 181 locomotive, as Irish Rail regard these as a common class.

B) Due to certain operating preferences, the following assumptions should be made:
(1) All passenger services from Dublin Heuston shown as booked either a class 001 or class 141 locomotive will be hauled by a class 071 locomotive if one is available, subject to any route restrictions.

(2) Most services shown booked as a class 001 locomotive will be hauled by a class 141/181 locomotive if one is available.

(3) Class 001 locomotives are preferred for all freight work except the overnight air braked liners and mail trains.

(4) There are no booked turns for the NIR 101 class locomotives, but they are used very occasionally on push/pull services vice multiple units, mainly between Portadown and Bangor.

The reporting numbers of trains scheduled to be formed of multiple unit stock are listed after the index of locomotive hauled trains.

Timetables

This section should be read in conjunction with the following publications:

NIR Timetable 1989–90 (from 15th May 1989 until further notice).
IR Mainline Timetable (from 15th May 1989 until further notice).
IR Dublin Suburban Timetable (from 15th May 1989 until further notice).

The times and services shown are those operative as at 15th May 1989.

TRAIN IDENTIFICATION NUMBERS

IRISH RAIL

IR utilise a system of four character train identification numbers, similar to those used on BR, to describe the nature and destination of all traffic over the network.

The train identification number is made up as follows:

1st digit

A single letter which describes the nature of the traffic conveyed as follows:

A - Mainline Passenger.
B - Mainline Passenger Specials.
C - Empty Diesel Suburban (Outer Destinations).
D - Diesel Suburban (Outer Destinations).
E - Electric.
F - Empty Electric.
H - Loose coupled movements.
I - Shunting. (See below)
J - Empty Mainline Passenger.
K - Chemical Laden & Empty.
L - Oil Laden & Empty.
M - Mineral Laden & Empty.
N - Cement Laden & Empty.
O - Stationary Vehicles. (Signalman's use only).
P - Diesel Suburban (Inner Destinations).
Q - Empty Diesel Suburban (Inner Destinations).
R - Light Engines.
S - Sundries/Unit Load Laden & Empty.
T - Fertiliser Laden & Empty.
U - Testing of Radio Equipment.
V - Beet Laden & Empty.
W - Departmental Trains Laden & Empty.
X - PW Machines & Cars capable of operating track circuits.
Y - PW Machines & Cars NOT capable of operating track circuits.
Z - Unusual Movements.

The Suburban area for the purpose of train IDs covers the passenger lines bounded by Arklow, Dundalk, Howth & Maynooth. The Outer Suburban stations are Arklow to Greystones inclusive, Malahide to Dundalk inclusive, Clonsilla and Maynooth. Inner Suburban stations are Bray to Howth inclusive.

The Mainline area is defined as all station except the suburban area.

Code I will be used as follows:

(i) for all 'Pilot Engine' movements for which the last three digits of the reporting number will be in the range 001 to 299 inclusive, the number being the locomotive number. These moves will be manually routed by the signalman.

47

(ii) for all automatic routable movements with an interlocking on the Dublin Suburban with trains or train engines the last three digits of the reporting number will be in the range 300 upwards.

2nd digit
A single number indicating the route/area over which the train operates as follows:

Suburban Area Destinations

1 - Arklow/Wicklow/Greystones.
2 - Bray.
3 - Dalkey.
4 - Dun Laoghaire.
5 - Lansdowne Road.
6 - Pearse.
7 - Connolly.
8 - Howth Junction or Malahide/Dundalk.
9 - Howth or Clonsilla/Maynooth.
0 - Fairview Depot.

Mainline Destinations

1 - Belfast.
2 - Cork, Cabra, Inchicore or Heuston.
3 - Tralee.
4 - Limerick.
5 - Waterford.
6 - Rosslare.
7 - Galway.
8 - Westport.
9 - Sligo.
0 - North Wall.

Mainline trains to Connolly have as the second digit of their reporting number the number representing their origin. (i.e. 1 from Belfast, 6 from Rosslare etc.)

3rd & 4th digits

The individual train identity number. The last digit of Up trains will be an odd number and Down trains an even number. Cork – Tralee trains are numbered according to their direction of movement on the Tralee branch.

NORTHERN IRELAND RAILWAYS

The NIR utilises a system of three numeric digits only for their train identification numbers, but these have a prefix letter on cross border services so as to fit in with the IR system.

IR's NEW LIVERY

▲ 049 stands outside Inchicore Workshops following a repaint in Irish Rail corporate image livery.
Peter Jones

▼ 071 Class No. 088 heads a rake of Mark 3 coaches through Kildare with the 0805 Tralee – Dublin Heuston on 9th October 1988. Both loco and coaches are in the new colour scheme.
Jonathan Allen

OLD DIESELS

▲ 101 Class No. B105 running right past the signal box at Ennis in May 1971. *Jonathan Allen*
▼ 113 Class No. B114 in April 1987 during it's time in the Inchicore Barrier. This locomotive has now been purchased for preservation by Westrail. *Andrew Marshall*

SMALL GMs

▲ **121 Class Nos. 129 & 122 provide unusual motive power for the 1500 Belfast Central — Dublin Connolly as the train leaves Lisburn on 24th July 1988.** *Jonathan Allen*

▼ **The driver changes ends after running round at Mallow with a Cork — Tralee service headed by 141 Class No. B159 in May 1971.** *Jonathan Allen*

DIESELS OLD & NEW

▲ 181 Class No. 187 heads a Werkspoor/Dundalk Boiler/Generator van and two CIE/Park Royal coaches forming the 1520 Limerick Junction – Limerick service on 14th May 1988. *Jonathan Allen*

▼ 401 Class No. E402 shunts postal vehicles at Dublin Heuston in April 1971. *Jonathan Allen*

▲ The remains of 201 Class No. B201 at Inchicore Works in 1973 following the bomb incident at Meigh on 15th August of that year. *Jonathan Allen*

▼ 201 Class No. 205 stands at Inchicore Works awaiting its fate in March 1987. This locomotive now forms part of the line of locos adjacent to the up side of the main line alongside the works which form a sound barrier for nearby houses. *Andrew Marshall*

PAST & PRESENT

▲ A CIE dmu headed by 2625 at Howth in May 1971. This line is now electrified and all trains are provided by DART emus.   *Jonathan Allen*

▼ Emu 8120 & 8320 departs from Dublin Pearse on a Howth – Bray working.   *Bernard McDonagh*

▲ Looking smart in its two tone green livery, preserved 421 Class No. 421 shunts coaches at the Downpatrick & Ardglass Railway on 21st August 1988. *Peter Jones*

▼ Restored to CIE colours of the sixties, 421 Class No. E428 backs onto the stock prior to a run from Claremorris to Ballina with a special working on 3rd April 1988. *Peter Jones*

DEUTZ SHUNTERS

▲ 611 Class No. G615 stands alongside 201 Class No. B233 at Inchicore in 1973. The shunter has now been broken up after a spell spent working for the Irish Sugar Company at Thurles.

Jonathan Allen

▼ 611 Class No. G611 inside Limerick Wagon Works from whence it has been purchased for preservation by the Great Southern Railway Preservation Society. *Peter Jones*

▲ Push/Pull Driving Brake Generator Open Standard No. 6101 at Drogheda on a test run on 11th February 1988. *Peter Jones*

▼ Mark 3 Open Standard No. 7129 at Inchicore shortly after delivery in March 1987. *Andrew Marshall*

RED DIESELS

▲ 1 Class shunter No. 1 is now preserved by the NIR at Lisburn as a static exhibit, where it is seen on 10th September 1989. *Chris Walker*

▼ In original livery, 101 Class No. 102 "FALCON" at Dublin Connolly with the "Enterprise" express service for Belfast Central in April 1971. *Jonathan Allen*

BLUE DIESELS

▲ **101 Class No. 102 "FALCON" departs from Belfast Central Services Depot on 30th September 1988.** *Hugh Ballantyne*

▼ **104 Class No. 104 aids a failed 80 class dmu at Lisburn on 9th April 1988.** *Jonathan Allen*

GLENS & CASTLES

▲ An 80 Class dmu with DMBSO No. 93 leading arrives at Belfast Central with the 1105 Bangor to Lisburn on 28th September 1988. This set is painted in NIR suburban sector livery. A number of the InterCity sector cars are named after Glens.   *Hugh Ballantyne*

▼ Castle Class dmu with DTSO 781 leading departs from Larne Harbour with the 1450 to Belfast York Road on 13th August 1988.   *Jonathan Allen*

RIVER CLASS

▲ River Class dmu formed DMSO 72 & TSK 725 & DTBSO 701 in Sealink livery at Whiteabbey with a Larne Harbour service in October 1983. *Jonathan Allen*

▼ River Class dmu with DTBSO 703 leading at Jordanstown with a Larne Harbour to Belfast York Road working in 1974. *Jonathan Allen*

MEDs & MPDs

▲ MED 3 car dmu headed by DMSO No. 17 leaves Lisburn with a Portadown service in 1972.
Jonathan Allen

▼ MPD 3 car dmu headed by DMBSO No. 52 at Antrim with a service to Belfast York Road during 1980, the last year of service of these cars.
Jonathan Allen

▲ NCC Railcar No. 1 at Ballymena in 1974, still carrying UTA livery. This vehicle is currently at Whitehead awaiting restoration.   *Jonathan Allen*

▼ Former GNR (I) railcar No. 134 at Belfast Great Victoria Street station in April 1971.
                                                                    Jonathan Allen

BLUE & GREY

▲ 111 Class No. 113 "BELFAST & Co. DOWN" at Belfast Central Services depot on 30th September 1988.   *Hugh Ballantyne*

▼ FO No. 904 entered service with NIR on 21st January 1989 still carrying BR livery. It is seen here at Dublin Connolly sandwiched between two vehicles in NIR InterCity livery.   *Chris Walker*

LIST OF LOCOMOTIVE DIAGRAMS

IR 001 CLASS.

Irish Rail's largest and oldest class of locomotives are soon to enter their thirty–fifth year of service. There has been little change in their use on passenger services in recent years they being mainly confined to local services in the Cork and Dublin suburban areas deputising for 141 & 181 class locos. The only regular booked mainline passenger duties for this class are confined to the Dublin Connolly to Rosslare Harbour services, and a daily working between Dublin Heuston and Waterford. These locomotives are still regular performers on freight services throughout the Irish Rail system and also occasionally in Northern Ireland on cross border services to/from Adelaide Yard (near Belfast).

001.01:	1100	FO	Dublin Heuston–Galway
	1510	FO	Galway–Dublin Heuston
	2050	FO	Dublin Heuston–Cork
001.02:	0700	SX	Dublin Connolly–Maynooth
	0815	SX	Maynooth–Dublin Connolly
	0935		Dublin Connolly–Rosslare Harbour Pier
	1455		Rosslare Harbour Pier–Dublin Connolly
	1830		Dublin Connolly–Rosslare Harbour Pier
001.03:	0755		Rosslare Harbour Pier–Dublin Connolly
	1335		Dublin Connolly–Rosslare Harbour Pier
	1800		Rosslare Harbour Pier–Dublin Connolly
001.04:	1505		Dublin Heuston–Waterford
	1820		Waterford–Dublin Heuston
001.05:	1245		Cork–Tralee
	1735		Tralee–Cork
	2000		Cork–Mallow
	2045	FX	Mallow–Cork
001.06:	1700	FO	Dublin Heuston–Ballina
001.07:	1030	SUN	Dublin Connolly–Belfast Central
	1500	SUN	Belfast Central–Dublin Connolly
001.08:	1150*	SUN	Claremorris–Ballina
	1250*	SUN	Claremorris–Ballina
	1530	SUN	Ballina–Dublin Heuston
001.09:	1025	SUN	Dublin Connolly–Rosslare Harbour Pier
	1800	SUN	Rosslare Harbour Pier–Dublin Connolly
001.10:	0915	SUN	Rosslare Harbour Pier–Dublin Connolly
	1805	SUN	Dublin Connolly–Rosslare Harbour Pier

IR 071 CLASS.

These locomotives are the pride of Irish Rail's fleet working the vast majority of express passenger services to and from Dublin Heuston on routes to the south and west and also on the Dublin Connolly to Belfast route in conjunction with the NIR whose class 111 locomotives are identical. Class 071 locomotives are very rarely seen on freight services other than overnight liner trains.

071.01:	0730	SX	Dublin Heuston–Cork
	0820	SO	Dublin Heuston–Cork
	1135		Cork–Dublin Heuston
	1825	FX	Dublin Heuston–Tralee
	1830	FO	Dublin Heuston–Tralee
071.02:	0730		Tralee–Dublin Heuston
	1440		Dublin Heuston–Cork
	1850		Cork–Dublin Heuston
071.03:	0530	MO	Dublin Heuston–Cork
	0800	MX	Mallow–Cork
	0900		Cork–Dublin Heuston
	1740		Dublin Heuston–Limerick
071.04:	0740		Dublin Heuston–Waterford
	1050		Waterford–Dublin Heuston
	1730		Dublin Heuston–Cork

071.05:	0800		Dublin Connolly–Belfast Central
	1100		Belfast Central–Dublin Connolly
	1500		Dublin Connolly–Belfast Central
	1800		Belfast Central–Dublin Connolly
071.06:	0800		Galway–Dublin Heuston
	1315		Dublin Heuston–Westport
	1815		Westport–Dublin Heuston
071.07:	0755		Dublin Heuston–Galway
	1135		Galway–Dublin Heuston
	1805		Dublin Heuston–Westport
071.08:	0730		Westport–Dublin Heuston
	1405		Dublin Heuston–Galway
	1825		Galway–Dublin Heuston
071.09:	0730		Cork–Dublin Heuston
	1135		Dublin Heuston–Waterford
	1525		Waterford–Dublin Heuston
071.10:	0555	MO	Limerick–Limerick Junction
	0730	MO	Limerick Junction–Limerick
	0830		Limerick–Dublin Heuston
	1300		Dublin Heuston–Cork
	1730		Cork–Dublin Heuston
	2050	FX	Dublin Heuston–Cork
071.11:	0520		Cork–Dublin Heuston
	1040		Dublin Heuston–Cork
	1445		Cork–Dublin Heuston
	1850		Dublin Heuston–Cork
071.12:	0840		Dublin Heuston–Tralee
	1425		Tralee–Dublin Heuston
071.13:	0740		Waterford–Dublin Heuston
	1100	FX	Dublin Heuston–Galway
	1510	FX	Galway–Dublin Heuston
	1645	FO	Dublin Heuston–Cork
071.14:	1810		Dublin Heuston–Waterford
071.15:	0830		Dublin Heuston–Westport
	1340		Westport–Dublin Heuston
	1835		Dublin Heuston–Galway
071.16:	0850	SUN	Dublin Heuston–Tralee
	1725	SUN	Tralee–Dublin Heuston
071.17:	0930	SUN	Dublin Heuston–Galway
	1810	SUN	Galway–Dublin Heuston
071.18:	1015	SUN	Dublin Heuston–Cork
	1430	SUN	Cork–Dublin Heuston
	1910	SUN	Dublin Heuston–Tralee
071.19:	1840	SUN	Dublin Heuston–Limerick
071.20:	0910*	SUN	Westport–Dublin Heuston
	1800	SUN	Dublin Heuston–Westport
071.21:	1830	SUN	Dublin Heuston–Cork
071.22:	0915	SUN	Cork–Dublin Heuston
	1350	SUN	Dublin Heuston–Cork
	1820	SUN	Cork–Dublin Heuston
071.23:	1845	SUN	Cork–Dublin Heuston
071.24:	1335	SUN	Tralee–Dublin Heuston
	2125	SUN	Dublin Heuston–Cork
071.25:	1750	SUN	Limerick–Dublin Heuston
071.26:	0950	SUN	Waterford–Dublin Heuston
	1820	SUN	Dublin Heuston–Waterford
071.27:	0905	SUN	Galway–Dublin Heuston
	1850	SUN	Dublin Heuston–Galway
071.28:	0800*	SUN	Westport–Athlone
	0830*	SUN	Dublin Heuston–Westport
	1118*	SUN	Athlone–Westport
	1750	SUN	Westport–Dublin Heuston
071.29:	1500	SUN	Dublin Connolly–Belfast Central
	1800	SUN	Belfast Central–Dublin Connolly

IR 121 CLASS.

This class of locomotives have seen a new lease of life since the introduction of the new Mark 3 push–pull sets on the Dublin Outer Suburban services. All locomotives have now been fitted with air brakes and can now be seen all over the Irish Rail system on all types of traffic. Visits to Northern Ireland are now becoming a regular occurence since the training of Connolly depot drivers on this class in connection with push–pull services to/from Dundalk. Being of a single cab design, they are normally used in pairs due to poor visibility available to the driver when running nose first. However, a single locomotive is required for the mark 3 push/pull services, with the nose end being marshalled against the train.

121.01:	0815		Dublin Connolly–Sligo
(2 x	1335		Sligo–Dublin Connolly
121)	1830		Dublin Connolly–Sligo
121.02:	0735		Sligo–Dublin Connolly
(2 x	1340		Dublin Connolly–Sligo
121)	1820		Sligo–Dublin Connolly
121.03:	0550		Dublin Heuston–Cork
	1500		Cork–Dublin Heuston
121.04:	0550	SX	Dundalk–Dublin Pearse
(P/P)	0806	SX	Dublin Pearse–Dundalk
	1046		Dundalk–Dublin Connolly
	1539		Dublin Pearse–Drogheda
	1700		Drogheda–Dublin Pearse
	1825		Dublin Pearse–Dundalk
121.05:	0724		Dundalk–Dublin Pearse
(P/P)	1325		Dublin Pearse–Drogheda
	1503		Drogheda–Dublin Pearse
	1730	SO	Dublin Pearse–Drogheda
	1743	SX	Dublin Pearse–Drogheda
121.06:	0716	SX	Drogheda–Dublin Pearse
(P/P)	1055	SX	Dublin Pearse–Dundalk
	1245	FO	Dundalk–Dublin Connolly
	1245	FSX	Dundalk–Dublin Pearse
	1715	SX	Dublin Pearse–Dundalk
121.07:	0731	SO	Drogheda–Dublin Pearse
(P/P)	0927	SO	Dublin Pearse–Drogheda
	1155	SO	Drogheda–Dublin Connolly
	1715	SO	Dublin Pearse–Dundalk
121.08:	0915	SUN	Dublin Connolly–Sligo
(2 x	1800	SUN	Sligo–Dublin Connolly
121)			
121.09:	0920	SUN	Sligo–Dublin Connolly
(2 x	1815	SUN	Dublin Connolly–Sligo
121)			

IR 141/181 CLASSES.

These two classes are regarded as a common fleet by Irish Rail and work the majority of suburban branch line passenger and local freight services throughout the system. They are also the most common type on cross–border freight services to/from Belfast.

141.01:	0634	SX	Dundalk–Dublin Pearse
	0808	SO	Dundalk–Dublin Pearse
	0927	SX	Dublin Pearse–Dundalk
	1055	SO	Dublin Pearse–Drogheda
	1155	SX	Drogheda–Dublin Connolly
	1245	SO	Dundalk–Dublin Connolly
	1632		Dublin Connolly–Drogheda
	1740		Drogheda–Dublin Connolly
	1905		Dublin Connolly–Dundalk
	2045	SX	Dundalk–Dublin Connolly

141.02:	0656	SO	Arklow–Mosney
	0808	SX	Dundalk–Dublin Pearse
	0945	SO	Mosney–Dublin Connolly
	1255		Dublin Pearse–Drogheda
	1414		Drogheda–Dublin Pearse
	1657		Dublin Pearse–Drogheda
	1815		Drogheda–Dublin Connolly
141.03:	0615	SX	Dublin Connolly–Drogheda
	0731	SX	Drogheda–Dublin Pearse
	1730	SX	Dublin Pearse–Drogheda
	1852	SX	Drogheda–Dublin Connolly
	2150	SX	Dublin Connolly–Dundalk
141.04:	0907	SX	Dublin Connolly–Maynooth
	0955	SX	Maynooth–Dublin Connolly
	1140		Dublin Connolly–Mosney
	1251		Mosney–Dublin Pearse
	1509		Dublin Pearse–Mosney
	1613		Mosney–Dublin Connolly
	1725	SX	Dublin Connolly–Arklow
141.05:	0656	SX	Arklow–Mosney
	0945	SX	Mosney–Dublin Connolly
141.06:	0500	MO	Sligo–Dublin Connolly
	0705	MSX	Mullingar–Dublin Connolly
141.07:	1715	FSX	Dublin Connolly–Mullingar
	1715	FO	Dublin Connolly–Sligo
141.08:	0700		Limerick–Dublin Heuston
(2 x	1745	FX	Dublin Heuston–Limerick Junction
141)	1745	FO	Dublin Heuston–Tralee
	2048	FX	Limerick Junction–Limerick
141.09:	0720		Ballina–Manulla Junction
	1142		Manulla Junction–Ballina
	1330		Ballina–Manulla Junction
	1627		Manulla Junction–Ballina
	1800		Ballina–Manulla Junction
	2107		Manulla Junction–Ballina
141.10:	0720		Cork–Cobh
	0755		Cobh–Cork
	0820		Cork–Mallow
	0910		Mallow–Cork
	1040		Cork–Mallow
	1122		Mallow–Cork
	1610		Mallow–Cork
141.11:	1010		Tralee–Cork
	1355*		Cork–Cobh
	1430*		Cobh–Cork
	1515		Cork–Tralee
141.12:	0655		Cobh–Cork
	0750		Cork–Cobh
	0825		Cobh–Cork
	0900		Cork–Cobh
	0935		Cobh–Cork
	1010		Cork–Cobh
	1045		Cobh–Cork
	1120		Cork–Cobh
	1200		Cobh–Cork
	1300		Cork–Cobh
	1345		Cobh–Cork
	1615*		Cork–Cobh
	1625*		Cork–Cobh
	1650*		Cobh–Cork
	1700*		Cobh–Cork
	1750		Cork–Cobh
	1820		Cobh–Cork
	1855		Cork–Cobh

	1930		Cobh–Cork
	2025		Cork–Cobh
	2100		Cobh–Cork
	2145		Cork–Cobh
	2220		Cobh–Cork
	2300		Cork–Cobh
	2335		Cobh–Cork
141.13:	0535	MO	Galway–Dublin Heuston
	0640	MSX	Athlone–Dublin Heuston
	1700	MSX	Dublin Heuston–Athlone
141.14:	1715	FO	Dublin Heuston–Waterford
141.15:	0600	MO	Waterford–Dublin Heuston
141.16:	0800		Limerick–Limerick Junction
	0903		Limerick Junction–Limerick
	1200		Limerick–Limerick Junction
	1248		Limerick Junction–Limerick
	1520		Limerick–Limerick Junction
	1635		Limerick Junction–Limerick
	1800		Limerick–Limerick Junction
	1840		Limerick Junction–Limerick
141.17:	0807		Limerick–Ballybrophy
	0950		Ballybrophy–Limerick
	1415		Limerick–Limerick Junction
	1455		Limerick Junction–Limerick
	1542		Limerick–Ballybrophy
	1908		Ballybrophy–Limerick
141.18:	0715*		Rosslare Harbour Pier–Limerick
	0920*	SO	Limerick–Limerick Junction
	0935*	SX	Limerick–Limerick Junction
	1035*		Limerick Junction–Limerick
	1535		Limerick–Rosslare Harbour Pier
141.19:	0715*		Rosslare Harbour Pier–Waterford
	0920*	SO	Limerick–Waterford
	0935*	SX	Limerick–Waterford
	1700		Waterford–Rosslare Harbour Pier
	1940		Rosslare Harbour Pier–Limerick
141.20:	1930		Limerick–Limerick Junction
	2010		Limerick Junction–Limerick
141.21:	2005	FO	Limerick–Limerick Junction
	2048	FO	Limerick Junction–Limerick
141.22:	2005	SUN	Dublin Heuston–Galway
141.23:	0955	SUN	Dublin Heuston–Waterford
(2 x	1805	SUN	Waterford–Dublin Heuston
141)			
141.24:	0940	SUN	Limerick–Ballybrophy
	1130	SUN	Ballybrophy–Limerick
	1730	SUN	Limerick–Ballybrophy
	1955	SUN	Ballybrophy–Limerick
141.25:	0955	SUN	Limerick–Limerick Junction
	1042	SUN	Limerick Junction–Limerick
	1135	SUN	Limerick–Limerick Junction
	1215	SUN	Limerick Junction–Limerick
	1500	SUN	Limerick–Limerick Junction
	1555	SUN	Limerick Junction–Limerick
141.26:	1920	SUN	Limerick–Limerick Junction
	1958	SUN	Limerick Junction–Limerick
141.27:	2000	SUN	Limerick–Limerick Junction
	2045	SUN	Limerick Junction–Limerick
	2327	SUN	Limerick Junction–Limerick
141.28:	1220	SUN	Cork–Tralee
	1750	SUN	Tralee–Cork
	2055	SUN	Cork–Mallow
	2135	SUN	Mallow–Cork

```
141.29:  1225  SUN  Cork–Cobh
         1300  SUN  Cobh–Cork
         1340  SUN  Cork–Cobh
         1415  SUN  Cobh–Cork
         1450  SUN  Cork–Cobh
         1525  SUN  Cobh–Cork
         1645  SUN  Cork–Cobh
         1730  SUN  Cobh–Cork
         1830  SUN  Cork–Cobh
         1905  SUN  Cobh–Cork
         2130  SUN  Cork–Cobh
         2205  SUN  Cobh–Cork
         2300  SUN  Cork–Cobh
         2335  SUN  Cobh–Cork
141.30:  0805  SUN  Tralee–Cork
         1050  SUN  Cork–Mallow
         1130  SUN  Mallow–Cork
```

NIR 101 CLASS.

This class formerly the mainstay of the cross–border Belfast–Dublin "Enterprise" service are now relegated to very occasional use on push–pull services mainly between Portadown and Bangor. They operate on services in place of multiple unit stock and therefore have no regular diagrams. These are the only locomotives throughout Ireland to be fitted with train heating equipment and hence do not need a generator van in the coaching stock formation. Visits to the Irish Republic are now very rare. This class is expected to be withdrawn from service by March 1990.

NIR 104 CLASS.

These locomotives were purchased by the NIR from CIE in 1986 for freight work. Being vacuum braked only they cannot work passenger services in Northern Ireland as all passenger stock is air braked only. However plans have now been drawn up for installing air brakes and buckeye couplings on these locomotives so future workings may soon be a possibility. Visits to the Irish Republic are very rare.

NIR 111 CLASS.

Identical to I.R's 071 class this class is the most intensively used in the whole of Ireland there being two daily passenger diagrams on the Belfast to Dublin route for the class of three locomotives.

```
111.01:  0800        Belfast Central–Dublin Connolly
         1100        Dublin Connolly–Belfast Central
         1500        Belfast Central–Dublin Connolly
         1820        Dublin Connolly–Belfast Central
111.02:  0700  SX    Belfast Central–Portadown
         0800  SX    Portadown–Belfast Central
         0900        Belfast Central–Dublin Connolly
         1300        Dublin Connolly–Belfast Central
         1700        Belfast Central–Dublin Connolly
         2015        Dublin Connolly–Belfast Central
111.03:  1015  SUN   Belfast Central–Dublin Connolly
         1820  SUN   Dublin Connolly–Belfast Central
111.04:  1700  SUN   Belfast Central–Dublin Connolly
         1950  SUN   Dublin Connolly–Belfast Central
```

INDEX OF LOCOMOTIVE HAULED TRAINS

Arklow

A607	0656	SO	Mosney	141.02
A607	0656	SX	Mosney	141.05

Athlone

A701	0640	MSX	Dublin Heuston	141.13
A872	1118	SUN	Westport	071.28

Ballina

A831	0720		Manulla Junction	141.09
A837	1330		Manulla Junction	141.09
A873	1530	SUN	Dublin Heuston	001.08
A843	1800		Manulla Junction	141.09

Ballybrophy

A402	0950		Limerick	141.17
A470	1130	SUN	Limerick	141.24
A410	1908		Limerick	141.17
A478	1955	SUN	Limerick	141.24

Belfast Central

303	0700	SX	Portadown	111.02
A121	0800		Dublin Connolly	111.01
A123	0900		Dublin Connolly	111.02
A171	1015	SUN	Dublin Connolly	111.03
A125	1100		Dublin Connolly	071.05
A135	1500		Dublin Connolly	111.01
A175	1500	SUN	Dublin Connolly	001.07
A177	1700	SUN	Dublin Connolly	111.04
A141	1700		Dublin Connolly	111.02
A143	1800		Dublin Connolly	071.05
A179	1800	SUN	Dublin Connolly	071.29

Claremorris

A880	1150	SUN	Ballina	001.08
A882	1250	SUN	Ballina	001.08

Cobh

D201	0655		Cork	141.12
D203	0755		Cork	141.10
D205	0825		Cork	141.12
D207	0935		Cork	141.12
D209	1045		Cork	141.12
D211	1200		Cork	141.12
D283	1300	SUN	Cork	141.29
D213	1345		Cork	141.12
D285	1415	SUN	Cork	141.29
D215	1430		Cork	141.11
D287	1525	SUN	Cork	141.29
D217	1650		Cork	141.12
D217	1700		Cork	141.12
D291	1730	SUN	Cork	141.29
D221	1820		Cork	141.12
D293	1905	SUN	Cork	141.29

D225	1930		Cork	141.12
D227	2100		Cork	141.12
D295	2205	SUN	Cork	141.29
D229	2220		Cork	141.12
D231	2335		Cork	141.12
D297	2335	SUN	Cork	141.29

Cork

A201	0520		Dublin Heuston	071.11
D204	0720		Cobh	141.10
A203	0730		Dublin Heuston	071.09
D206	0750		Cobh	141.12
A233	0820		Mallow	141.10
A207	0900		Dublin Heuston	071.03
D208	0900		Cobh	141.12
A271	0915	SUN	Dublin Heuston	071.22
D210	1010		Cobh	141.12
A235	1040		Mallow	141.10
A273	1050	SUN	Mallow	141.30
D212	1120		Cobh	141.12
A211	1135		Dublin Heuston	071.01
A374	1220	SUN	Tralee	141.28
D282	1225	SUN	Cobh	141.29
A304	1245		Tralee	001.05
D214	1300		Cobh	141.12
D284	1340	SUN	Cobh	141.29
D216	1355		Cobh	141.11
A275	1430	SUN	Dublin Heuston	071.18
A215	1445		Dublin Heuston	071.11
D286	1450	SUN	Cobh	141.29
A281	1500		Dublin Heuston	121.03
A312	1515		Tralee	141.11
D220	1615		Cobh	141.12
D220	1625		Cobh	141.12
D290	1645	SUN	Cobh	141.29
A221	1730		Dublin Heuston	071.10
D222	1750		Cobh	141.12
A277	1820	SUN	Dublin Heuston	071.22
D292	1830	SUN	Cobh	141.29
A279	1845	SUN	Dublin Heuston	071.23
A223	1850		Dublin Heuston	071.02
D226	1855		Cobh	141.12
A243	2000		Mallow	001.05
A283	2055	SUN	Mallow	141.28
D294	2130	SUN	Cobh	141.29
D230	2145		Cobh	141.12
D232	2300		Cobh	141.12
D296	2300	SUN	Cobh	141.29

Drogheda

P603	0716	SX	Dublin Pearse	121.06
P604	0731	SO	Dublin Pearse	121.07
P604	0731	SX	Dublin Pearse	141.03
P713	1155	SO	Dublin Connolly	121.07
P713	1155	SX	Dublin Connolly	141.01
P617	1414		Dublin Pearse	141.02
P618	1503		Dublin Pearse	121.05
P621	1700		Dublin Pearse	121.04
P722	1740		Dublin Connolly	141.01

71

P723 1815 Dublin Connolly 141.02
P724 1852 SX Dublin Connolly 141.03

Dublin Connolly

D801	0615	SX	Drogheda	141.03
D902	0700	SX	Maynooth	001.02
A124	0800		Belfast Central	071.05
A900	0815		Sligo	121.01
D906	0907	SX	Maynooth	141.04
A970	0915	SUN	Sligo	121.08
A600	0935		Rosslare Hbr. Pier	001.02
A606	1025	SUN	Rosslare Hbr. Pier	001.09
A170	1030	SUN	Belfast Central	001.07
A132	1100		Belfast Central	111.01
D810	1140		Mosney	141.04
A136	1300		Belfast Central	111.02
A602	1335		Rosslare Hbr. Pier	001.03
A902	1340		Sligo	121.02
A136	1500		Belfast Central	071.05
A174	1500	SUN	Belfast Central	071.29
D817	1632		Drogheda	141.01
A906	1715	FO	Sligo	141.07
A908	1715	FSX	Mullingar	141.07
A610	1725	SX	Arklow	141.04
A608	1805	SUN	Rosslare Hbr. Pier	001.10
A976	1815	SUN	Sligo	121.09
A144	1820		Belfast Central	111.01
A176	1820	SUN	Belfast Central	111.03
A604	1830		Rosslare Hbr. Pier	001.02
A910	1830		Sligo	121.01
D823	1905		Dundalk	141.01
A178	1950	SUN	Belfast Central	111.04
A150	2015		Belfast Central	111.02
D826	2150	SX	Dundalk	141.03

Dublin Heuston

A230	0530	MO	Cork	071.03
A202	0550		Cork	121.03
A204	0730	SX	Cork	071.01
A500	0740		Waterford	071.04
A700	0755		Galway	071.07
A204	0820	SO	Cork	071.01
A800	0830		Westport	071.15
A870	0830	SUN	Westport	071.28
A302	0840		Tralee	071.12
A370	0850	SUN	Tralee	071.16
A770	0930	SUN	Galway	071.17
A572	0955	SUN	Waterford	141.23
A272	1015	SUN	Cork	071.18
A208	1040		Cork	071.11
A706	1100	FO	Galway	001.01
A706	1100	FX	Galway	071.13
A504	1135		Waterford	071.09
A212	1300		Cork	071.10
A806	1315		Westport	071.06
A274	1350	SUN	Cork	071.22
A710	1405		Galway	071.08
A214	1440		Cork	071.02
A508	1505		Waterford	001.04
A218	1645	FO	Cork	071.13
A810	1700	FO	Ballina	001.06
A810	1700	MSX	Athlone	141.13
A510	1715	FO	Waterford	141.14
A220	1730		Cork	071.04
A408	1740		Limerick	071.03
A318	1745	FO	Tralee	141.08
A416	1745	FX	Limerick Junction	141.08
A876	1800	SUN	Westport	071.20
A812	1805		Westport	071.07
A512	1810		Waterford	071.14
A578	1820	SUN	Waterford	071.26
A322	1825	FX	Tralee	071.01
A276	1830	SUN	Cork	071.21
A322	1830	FO	Tralee	071.01
A716	1835		Galway	071.15
A476	1840	SUN	Limerick	071.19
A224	1850		Cork	071.11
A776	1850	SUN	Galway	071.27
A376	1910	SUN	Tralee	071.18
A778	2005	SUN	Galway	141.23
A226	2050	FO	Cork	001.01
A226	2050	FX	Cork	071.10
A280	2125	SUN	Cork	071.24

Dublin Pearse

D804	0806	SX	Dundalk	121.04
D807	0927	SO	Drogheda	121.07
D807	0927	SX	Drogheda	141.01
D809	1055	SO	Dundalk	141.01
D809	1055	SX	Dundalk	121.06
D812	1255		Drogheda	141.02
D813	1325		Drogheda	121.05
D815	1509		Mosney	141.04
D816	1539		Drogheda	121.04
D818	1657		Drogheda	141.02
D819	1715	SO	Dundalk	121.07
D819	1715	SX	Dundalk	121.06
D820	1730	SO	Drogheda	121.05
D820	1730	SX	Drogheda	141.03
D821	1743	SX	Drogheda	121.05
D822	1825		Dundalk	121.04

Dundalk

P601	0550	SX	Dublin Pearse	121.04
P602	0634	SX	Dublin Pearse	141.01
P606	0724		Dublin Pearse	121.05
P608	0808	SO	Dublin Pearse	141.01
P608	0808	SX	Dublin Pearse	141.02
P712	1046		Dublin Connolly	121.04
P615	1245	FO	Dublin Connolly	121.06
P615	1245	FSX	Dublin Pearse	121.06
P615	1245	SO	Dublin Connolly	141.01
P727	2045	SX	Dublin Connolly	141.01

Galway

A701	0535	MO	Dublin Heuston	141.13
A703	0800		Dublin Heuston	071.06
A773	0905	SUN	Dublin Heuston	071.27
A707	1135		Dublin Heuston	071.07
A711	1510	FO	Dublin Heuston	001.01
A711	1510	FX	Dublin Heuston	071.13
A777	1810	SUN	Dublin Heuston	071.17

A717	1825		Dublin Heuston	071.08

Limerick

A422	0555	MO	Limerick Junction	071.10
A403	0700		Dublin Heuston	141.08
A424	0800		Limerick Junction	141.16
A401	0807		Ballybrophy	141.17
A405	0830		Dublin Heuston	071.10
A426	0920	SO	Limerick Junction	141.18
A450	0920	SO	Waterford	141.19
A426	0935	SX	Limerick Junction	141.18
A450	0935	SX	Waterford	141.19
A471	0940	SUN	Ballybrophy	141.24
A480	0955	SUN	Limerick Junction	141.25
A482	1135	SUN	Limerick Junction	141.25
A428	1200		Limerick Junction	141.16
A432	1415		Limerick Junction	141.17
A486	1500	SUN	Limerick Junction	141.25
A434	1520		Limerick Junction	141.16
A462	1535		Rosslare Hbr. Pier	141.18
A411	1542		Ballybrophy	141.17
A479	1730	SUN	Ballybrophy	141.24
A477	1750	SUN	Dublin Heuston	071.25
A438	1800		Limerick Junction	141.16
A490	1920	SUN	Limerick Junction	141.26
A442	1930		Limerick Junction	141.20
A492	2000	SUN	Limerick Junction	141.27
A444	2005	FO	Limerick Junction	141.21

Limerick Junction

A423	0730	MO	Limerick	071.10
A425	0903		Limerick	141.16
A427	1035		Limerick	141.18
A481	1042	SUN	Limerick	141.25
A483	1215	SUN	Limerick	141.25
A431	1248		Limerick	141.16
A433	1455		Limerick	141.17
A487	1555	SUN	Limerick	141.25
A435	1635		Limerick	141.16
A439	1840		Limerick	141.16
A489	1958	SUN	Limerick	141.26
A443	2010		Limerick	141.20
A491	2045	SUN	Limerick	141.27
A445	2048	FO	Limerick	141.21
A445	2048	FX	Limerick	141.08
A493	2327	SUN	Limerick	141.27

Mallow

A230	0800	MX	Cork	071.03
A232	0910		Cork	141.10
A234	1122		Cork	141.10
A270	1130	SUN	Cork	141.30
A282	1610		Cork	141.10
A222	2045	FX	Cork	001.05
A282	2135	SUN	Cork	141.28

Manulla Junction

A830	1142		Ballina	141.09
A836	1627		Ballina	141.09
A842	2107		Ballina	141.09

Maynooth

P733	0815	SX	Dublin Connolly	001.02
P737	0955	SX	Dublin Connolly	141.04

Mosney

P710	0945	SO	Dublin Connolly	141.02
P710	0945	SX	Dublin Connolly	141.05
P614	1251		Dublin Pearse	141.04
P720	1613		Dublin Connolly	141.04

Mullingar

A901	0705	MSX	Dublin Connolly	141.06

Portadown

310	0800	SX	Belfast Central	111.02

Rosslare Harbour Pier

A561	0715		Waterford	141.19
A461	0715		Limerick	141.18
A601	0755		Dublin Connolly	001.03
A671	0915	SUN	Dublin Connolly	001.10
A603	1455		Dublin Connolly	001.02
A605	1800		Dublin Connolly	001.03
A677	1800	SUN	Dublin Connolly	001.09
A463	1940		Limerick	141.19

Sligo

A901	0500	MO	Dublin Connolly	141.06
A903	0735		Dublin Connolly	121.02
A971	0920	SUN	Dublin Connolly	121.09
A905	1335		Dublin Connolly	121.01
A977	1800	SUN	Dublin Connolly	121.08
A907	1820		Dublin Connolly	121.02

Tralee

A301	0730		Dublin Heuston	071.02
A371	0805	SUN	Cork	141.30
A303	1010		Cork	141.11
A375	1335	SUN	Dublin Heuston	071.24
A307	1425		Dublin Heuston	071.12
A377	1725	SUN	Dublin Heuston	071.16
A311	1735		Cork	001.05
A379	1750	SUN	Cork	141.28

Waterford

A501	0600	MO	Dublin Heuston	141.15
A503	0740		Dublin Heuston	071.13
A575	0950	SUN	Dublin Heuston	071.26
A509	1050		Dublin Heuston	071.04
A511	1525		Dublin Heuston	071.09
A564	1700		Rosslare Hbr. Pier	141.19
A579	1805	SUN	Dublin Heuston	141.23
A517	1820		Dublin Heuston	001.04

73

Westport

A801	0730		Dublin Heuston	071.08
A871	0800	SUN	Athlone	071.28
A873	0910	SUN	Dublin Heuston	071.20
A807	1340		Dublin Heuston	071.15
A877	1750	SUN	Dublin Heuston	071.28
A813	1815		Dublin Heuston	071.06

DART TRAIN IDENTIFICATION NUMBERS

Bray

E903	0630	SX	Howth
E904	0650		Howth
E905	0700		Howth
E906	0710		Howth
E908	0730		Howth
E803	0740	SX	Howth Junction
E909	0740	SO	Howth
E807	0753	SX	Howth Junction
E913	0800		Howth
E808	0810	SX	Howth Junction
E915	0810	SO	Howth
E702	0815	SX	Dublin Connolly
E916	0820		Howth
E703	0825	SX	Dublin Connolly
E918	0830	SX	Howth
E705	0840	SX	Dublin Connolly
E919	0840	SO	Howth
E921	0850		Howth
E922	0905		Howth
E706	0915	SX	Dublin Connolly
E923	0915	SO	Howth
E924	0930		Howth
E902	0930	SUN	Howth
E925	0945		Howth
E926	0955		Howth
E903	1000	SUN	Howth
E927	1005		Howth
E928	1030		Howth
E904	1030	SUN	Howth
E929	1045		Howth
E930	1055		Howth
E905	1100	SUN	Howth
E931	1115		Howth
E932	1130		Howth
E906	1130	SUN	Howth
E933	1145		Howth
E934	1200		Howth
E907	1200	SUN	Howth
E935	1210		Howth
E908	1220	SUN	Howth
E937	1230		Howth
E909	1240	SUN	Howth
E938	1245		Howth
E939	1300		Howth
E910	1300	SUN	Howth
E940	1315		Howth
E911	1320	SUN	Howth
E941	1330		Howth
E912	1340	SUN	Howth
E942	1345		Howth

E943	1400		Howth
E913	1400	SUN	Howth
E944	1410		Howth
E914	1425	SUN	Howth
E946	1430		Howth
E915	1440	SUN	Howth
E947	1445		Howth
E948	1500		Howth
E916	1500	SUN	Howth
E949	1515		Howth
E917	1520	SUN	Howth
E950	1530		Howth
E918	1540	SUN	Howth
E951	1545		Howth
E952	1600		Howth
E919	1600	SUN	Howth
E953	1615		Howth
E920	1620	SUN	Howth
E955	1635		Howth
E921	1640	SUN	Howth
E956	1645		Howth
E958	1700		Howth
E922	1700	SUN	Howth
E959	1705	SX	Howth
E960	1715		Howth
E961	1720	SX	Howth
E923	1720	SUN	Howth
E962	1725		Howth
E924	1740	SUN	Howth
E963	1745		Howth
E964	1758		Howth
E925	1800	SUN	Howth
E711	1805	SX	Dublin Connolly
E712	1810	SX	Dublin Connolly
E966	1815		Howth
E926	1820	SUN	Howth
E967	1830		Howth
E968	1840		Howth
E927	1840	SUN	Howth
E714	1850		Dublin Connolly
E969	1900		Howth
E928	1900	SUN	Howth
E970	1910		Howth
E929	1920	SUN	Howth
E971	1930		Howth
E930	1940	SUN	Howth
E972	1945		Howth
E973	2000		Howth
E931	2000	SUN	Howth
E974	2015		Howth
E932	2020	SUN	Howth
E976	2035		Howth

E977	2045		Howth
E933	2045	SUN	Howth
E978	2100		Howth
E934	2100	SUN	Howth
E979	2115		Howth
E935	2120	SUN	Howth
E980	2130		Howth
E936	2140	SUN	Howth
E981	2145		Howth
E982	2200		Howth
E937	2200	SUN	Howth
E983	2215		Howth
E938	2220	SUN	Howth
E984	2230		Howth
E939	2240	SUN	Howth
E985	2245		Howth
E717	2300		Dublin Connolly
E707	2300	SUN	Dublin Connolly
E718	2315		Dublin Connolly

Dalkey

E811	1640	SX	Howth Junction

Dublin Connolly

E201	0646		Bray
E902	0655		Howth
E903	0707	SO	Howth
E204	0730	SX	Bray
E401	0800		Dun Laoghaire
E401	0800	SUN	Dun Laoghaire
E900	0935	SUN	Howth
E232	1256	SX	Bray
E301	1606	SX	Dalkey
E250	1621	SX	Bray
E411	1636	SX	Dun Laoghaire
E253	1651	SX	Bray
E256	1721	SX	Bray
E258	1736	SX	Bray
E262	1751	SX	Bray
E413	1756	SO	Dun Laoghaire
E416	1956		Dun Laoghaire

Dublin Pearse

E901	0635		Howth
E911	0823	SX	Howth

Dun Laoghaire

E701	0723		Dublin Connolly
E907	0740	SX	Howth
E914	0822	SX	Howth
E704	0846	SO	Dublin Connolly
E812	1705	SX	Howth Junction
E713	1845		Dublin Connolly

Howth

E202	0635	SX	Bray
E203	0655		Bray
E205	0715		Bray
E207	0730		Bray

E208	0745		Bray
E601	0755	SX	Dun Laoghaire
E210	0800		Bray
E211	0810		Bray
E212	0815	SX	Bray
E213	0825		Bray
E214	0835		Bray
E215	0850		Bray
E604	0905		Dublin Pearse
E217	0920		Bray
E218	0930		Bray
E200	0935	SUN	Bray
E219	0950		Bray
E220	1000		Bray
E201	1005	SUN	Bray
E221	1010		Bray
E222	1025		Bray
E202	1030	SUN	Bray
E223	1040		Bray
E224	1055		Bray
E203	1100	SUN	Bray
E225	1110		Bray
E226	1125		Bray
E204	1130	SUN	Bray
E227	1140		Bray
E228	1155		Bray
E205	1200	SUN	Bray
E229	1210		Bray
E231	1225		Bray
E206	1230	SUN	Bray
E233	1240		Bray
E207	1240	SUN	Bray
E234	1250		Bray
E208	1310	SUN	Bray
E236	1317		Bray
E237	1328		Bray
E209	1330	SUN	Bray
E238	1345		Bray
E210	1350	SUN	Bray
E239	1355		Bray
E241	1410		Bray
E211	1410	SUN	Bray
E242	1425		Bray
E212	1430	SUN	Bray
E243	1440		Bray
E213	1450	SUN	Bray
E244	1455		Bray
E245	1510		Bray
E214	1510	SUN	Bray
E246	1525		Bray
E215	1530	SUN	Bray
E247	1540		Bray
E216	1550	SUN	Bray
E249	1555		Bray
E251	1610		Bray
E217	1610	SUN	Bray
E252	1620		Bray
E218	1630	SUN	Bray
E254	1640		Bray
E255	1650		Bray
E219	1650	SUN	Bray
E257	1710		Bray
E220	1710	SUN	Bray
E261	1725		Bray

E281	2125		Bray
E233	2130	SUN	Bray
E282	2140		Bray
E234	2150	SUN	Bray
E283	2155		Bray
E284	2210		Bray
E235	2210	SUN	Bray
E285	2225		Bray
E236	2230	SUN	Bray
E286	2240		Bray
E237	2250	SUN	Bray
E287	2255		Bray
E721	2310		Dublin Connolly
E238	2310	SUN	Bray
E722	2325		Dublin Connolly
E715	2330	SUN	Dublin Connolly
E723	2345		Dublin Connolly
E716	2350	SUN	Dublin Connolly
E221	1725	SUN	Bray
E263	1740		Bray
E264	1750		Bray
E222	1750	SUN	Bray
E223	1810	SUN	Bray
E266	1815		Bray
E267	1825		Bray
E224	1830	SUN	Bray
E268	1840		Bray
E225	1850	SUN	Bray
E269	1855		Bray
E270	1905		Bray
E226	1910	SUN	Bray
E272	1925		Bray
E227	1935	SUN	Bray
E273	1945		Bray
E228	1950	SUN	Bray
E274	2000		Bray
E275	2010		Bray
E229	2015	SUN	Bray
E276	2025		Bray
E230	2030	SUN	Bray
E277	2040		Bray
E231	2050	SUN	Bray
E278	2055		Bray
E279	2105		Bray
E232	2110	SUN	Bray

Howth Junction

E206	0732	SX	Bray
E602	0837	SX	Dublin Pearse
E403	0852	SX	Dun Laoghaire
E404	0907	SX	Dun Laoghaire
E259	1727	SX	Bray
E413	1743	SX	Dun Laoghaire

IR MULTIPLE UNIT TRAIN IDENTIFICATION NUMBERS

Bray

D100   All local services to Greystones

Greystones

P200   All local services to Bray

Dublin Connolly

D900	0545	SX	Maynooth
D904	0825	SX	Maynooth
D909	1620	SX	Maynooth
D911	1755	SX	Maynooth

Maynooth

P731	0705	SX	Dublin Connolly
P735	0912	SX	Dublin Connolly
P744	1708	SX	Dublin Connolly
P747	1900	SX	Dublin Connolly

NIR TRAIN IDENTIFICATION NUMBERS

Adelaide

244	1407	SUN	Bangor
250	1606	SX	Bangor

Ballymena

410	1118	SX	Belfast Central
420	1439*	FSX	Belfast Central
420	1439*	SO	Bangor
430	1712	SO	Bangor

Bangor

307	0650	SX	Portadown
205	0700	SO	Lisburn
207	0710	SX	Lisburn
309	0730	SX	Portadown

209	0750	SX	Lisburn
211	0755	SX	Lisburn
311	0800	SO	Portadown
313	0815	SX	Portadown
213	0820	SX	Lisburn
215	0835	SX	Balmoral
217	0855	SX	Lisburn
405	0910	SX	Ballymena
315	0910	SO	Portadown
317	0935	SX	Portadown
219	0935	SUN	Belfast Central
319	0955	SO	Portadown
221	1005	SX	Lisburn
321	1035		Portadown
223	1105	SX	Lisburn
323	1120	SUN	Portadown
325	1135		Portadown
227	1205	SX	Lisburn

229	1220	SO	Lisburn
327	1235	SX	Portadown
413	1250	SO	Ballymena
231	1305	SX	Lisburn
231	1305	SUN	Belfast Central
329	1325	SO	Portadown
331	1335	SX	Portadown
235	1405	SX	Lisburn
419	1410	SO	Ballymena
333	1430	SUN	Portadown
421	1440	SX	Crumlin
335	1500	SO	Portadown
337	1505	SX	Portadown
339	1545	SX	Portadown
341	1550	SUN	Portadown
343	1555	SO	Portadown
345	1605	SX	Portadown
249	1635	SX	Lisburn
425	1635	SO	Portrush
349	1655	SX	Poyntzpass
347	1655	SUN	Portadown
351	1700		Portadown
251	1715	SX	Lisburn
429	1737	SX	Londonderry
253	1740	SX	Belfast Central
353	1745	SO	Dundalk
255	1755	SX	Lisburn
355	1755	SUN	Portadown
259	1815	SX	Lisburn
261	1825	SO	Lisburn
357	1845	FSX	Portadown
357	1845	FO	Newry
363	1905	SX	Portadown
361	1910	SO	Portadown
363	1925	SUN	Portadown
265	1935	SX	Belfast Central
365	2010		Portadown
367	2050		Portadown
369	2100	SUN	Portadown
267	2125		Lisburn
371	2220		Portadown

Belfast Central

201	0645	SX	Lisburn
208	0655	SX	Bangor
305	0705	SO	Portadown
401	0825		Londonderry
407	1010*		Portrush
407	1010*	FO	Portrush
407	1010	SUN	Londonderry
409	1130		Londonderry
411	1250	SX	Ballymena
240	1335	SUN	Bangor
417	1410		Londonderry
239	1540	SX	Lisburn
423	1610		Londonderry
243	1615	SO	Lisburn
245	1620	SX	Lisburn
252	1620	SUN	Bangor
427	1730	SX	Portrush
429	1805	SO	Londonderry
264	1807	SX	Bangor
147	1810	SX	Dundalk

431	1825	SUN	Portrush
433	2025	SX	Londonderry
435	2035	SO	Londonderry
437	2035*	SUN	Portrush
439	2105	SUN	Londonderry

Belfast York Road

701	0625	SX	Larne Harbour
801	0640	SO	Whitehead
703	0700		Larne Harbour
803	0710	SX	Whitehead
807	0750	SX	Whitehead
705	0750	SX	Larne Harbour
707	0805	SX	Larne Harbour
809	0815	SX	Whitehead
709	0835	SX	Larne Harbour
811	0835	SX	Whitehead
711	0900	SX	Larne Harbour
813	0920	SX	Whitehead
713	0920	SO	Larne Harbour
715	1000	SX	Larne Harbour
815	1005	SO	Whitehead
717	1030		Larne Harbour
717	1030*	SUN	Larne Harbour
817	1045	SX	Whitehead
819	1105	SX	Whitehead
719	1115	SO	Larne Harbour
721	1130	SUN	Larne Harbour
723	1135	SX	Larne Harbour
821	1205	SX	Whitehead
725	1215	SO	Larne Harbour
823	1230*	SUN	Whitehead
727	1235	SX	Larne Harbour
729	1300	SO	Larne Harbour
731	1320	SX	Larne Harbour
733	1330	SO	Larne Harbour
825	1400	SX	Whitehead
735	1400	SUN	Larne Harbour
737	1430		Larne Harbour
827	1440	SX	Whitehead
829	1445	SUN	Whitehead
831	1450	SO	Whitehead
833	1500	SX	Whitehead
739	1520		Larne Town
741	1540	SUN	Larne Harbour
835	1545	SX	Whitehead
743	1600		Larne Harbour
837	1620	SX	Whitehead
745	1640		Larne Harbour
747	1700	SX	Larne Town
749	1705	SO	Larne Harbour
839	1715	SX	Carrickfergus
841	1720	SUN	Whitehead
751	1730		Larne Harbour
843	1745	SX	Whitehead
753	1812		Larne Harbour
755	1830	7	Larne Harbour
757	1845	SX	Larne Harbour
845	1920	SX	Whitehead
759	1945	SO	Larne Harbour
761	1950	SX	Larne Harbour
763	2100	7	Larne Harbour
765	2215		Larne Harbour

Bridge End

237	1536	FO	Belfast Central
247	1636	SX	Lisburn

Carrickfergus

802	0740	SX	Belfast York Road
838	1737	SX	Belfast York Road

City Hospital

236	1226	SUN	Bangor

Coleraine

402	0605	SX	Bangor
503	0705	SX	Portrush
505	0800		Portrush
507	0848	SX	Portrush
507	0900	SO	Portrush
509	0920	SX	Portrush
511	1004		Portrush
513	1110		Portrush
515	1155*	FX	Portrush
515	1150*	SUN	Portrush
517	1310		Portrush
519	1400*	SUN	Portrush
519	1405*		Portrush
521	1440		Portrush
523	1529*	SX	University
525	1555		Portrush
527	1705		Portrush
527	1705*	SUN	Portrush
529	1755		Portrush
531	1810	SUN	Portrush
535	1915*	SUN	Portrush
531	1950	SX	Portrush
537	1950	SO	Portrush
533	2115	SX	Portrush
539	2115	SO	Portrush
541	2205*	SUN	Portrush
535	2217	SX	Portrush
541	2217	SO	Portrush
543	2245*	SUN	Portrush

Dundalk

148	2010		Bangor

Larne Harbour

702	0625		Belfast York Road
704	0653	SX	Belfast York Road
706	0740	SX	Belfast York Road
708	0800		Belfast York Road
710	0850	SO	Belfast York Road
712	0900	SX	Belfast York Road
714	0955		Belfast York Road
716	1000	SUN	Belfast York Road
718	1005	SX	Belfast York Road
720	1020	SO	Belfast York Road
722	1110		Belfast York Road
724	1130*	SUN	Belfast York Road

726	1205		Belfast York Road
728	1230	SUN	Belfast York Road
730	1300	SX	Belfast York Road
732	1310	SO	Belfast York Road
734	1350	SX	Belfast York Road
736	1355	SO	Belfast York Road
738	1420		Belfast York Road
740	1450	SUN	Belfast York Road
742	1520		Belfast York Road
746	1630	SUN	Belfast York Road
748	1653	SX	Belfast York Road
750	1705	SO	Belfast York Road
752	1730		Belfast York Road
756	1825		Belfast York Road
758	1910	SX	Belfast York Road
760	1915	SO	Belfast York Road
762	1940	SUN	Belfast York Road
764	1955	SX	Belfast York Road
766	2100		Belfast York Road
768	2150	7	Belfast York Road

Larne Town

744	1610		Belfast York Road
754	1755	SX	Belfast York Road

Lisburn

212	0710	SX	Bangor
216	0750	SX	Belfast Central
218	0810	SX	Bangor
220	0815	SO	Belfast Central
222	0845	SX	Belfast Central
226	0905	SX	Belfast Central
230	0920	SX	Belfast Central
224	0945	SX	Bangor
234	1120	SX	Bangor
238	1220	SX	Bangor
242	1320		Bangor
246	1420	SX	Bangor
248	1530	SX	Bangor
254	1618	SX	Bangor
424	1630	SX	Bangor
256	1635	SO	Bangor
258	1653	SX	Bangor
260	1710	SX	Bangor
262	1738	SX	Belfast Central
266	1820	SX	Bangor
270	1850	SX	Bangor
270	1930	SX	Bangor
264	1930	SO	Bangor
274	2235		Bangor

Londonderry

404	0620	SX	Belfast Central
404	0620	SO	Bangor
406	0800		Belfast Central
412	1105	7	Belfast Central
418	1405*	SUN	Portrush
426	1440		Belfast Central
432	1705		Belfast Central
434	1720	SUN	Belfast Central
438	1900*		Coleraine

78

442	1900*		Belfast Central

Newry

312	0730	SX	Bangor
312	0730	SO	Belfast Central
374	1955	SUN	Bangor

Portadown

302	0625	SX	Bangor
304	0655	SO	Bangor
306	0700	SX	Bangor
308	0735	SX	Bangor
314	0830	SX	Bangor
316	0900	SO	Bangor
318	0910	SX	Bangor
320	0950	SUN	Bangor
322	0955		Bangor
324	1035	SX	Bangor
326	1100	SO	Bangor
328	1135	SX	Bangor
330	1155	SO	Bangor
332	1230	SX	Bangor
334	1300	SO	Bangor
336	1325	SX	Bangor
338	1355	SO	Bangor
340	1400	SUN	Bangor
342	1425	SX	Bangor
344	1525	SO	Bangor
346	1530	SX	Bangor
348	1620	SUN	Bangor
350	1635	SX	Bangor
352	1655	SO	Bangor
354	1705	SX	Bangor
356	1735	SUN	Bangor
358	1745	SX	Bangor
360	1815	SO	Bangor
364	1850	SX	Belfast Central
366	1915	SUN	Bangor
368	1955	SX	Bangor
370	2000	SO	Bangor
372	2015	SUN	Belfast Central
378	2035	SX	Bangor

Portrush

502	0645		Coleraine
504	0725	SX	Coleraine
506	0825		Coleraine
508	0905	SX	Coleraine
408	0920	SO	Bangor
510	0940	SX	Coleraine

512	1020		Coleraine
514	1130		Coleraine
516	1245		Coleraine
518	1300*	SUN	Coleraine
416	1345*	SX	Belfast Central
416	1345*	SO	Bangor
520	1345*	FX	Coleraine
416	1345*	FO	Belfast Central
522	1420*	SUN	Coleraine
522	1421*		Coleraine
524	1505		Coleraine
528	1600*	SUN	Coleraine
530	1610	SO	Coleraine
530	1615	SX	Coleraine
532	1730		Coleraine
534	1745*	SUN	Coleraine
534	1830		Coleraine
436	1835	SUN	Belfast Central
440	1930*		Belfast Central
536	1930*		Coleraine
433	1950*	SUN	Londonderry
538	2030	7	Coleraine
540	2155	SX	Coleraine
542	2155	SO	Coleraine
542	2223	SUN	Coleraine
544	2235		Coleraine
546	2301	SUN	Coleraine

Whitehead

804	0745	SX	Belfast York Road
806	0750	SO	Belfast York Road
808	0821	SX	Belfast York Road
810	0847	SX	Belfast York Road
812	0930	SO	Belfast York Road
814	0955	SX	Belfast York Road
816	1100	SO	Belfast York Road
818	1155		Belfast York Road
820	1255	SX	Belfast York Road
822	1345*	SUN	Belfast York Road
824	1450	SX	Belfast York Road
826	1520	SX	Belfast York Road
828	1525	SO	Belfast York Road
830	1545*	SUN	Belfast York Road
832	1555	SX	Belfast York Road
834	1620	SX	Belfast York Road
836	1655	SX	Belfast York Road
840	1751	SUN	Belfast York Road
842	1855	SX	Belfast York Road
844	1955	SX	Belfast York Road

University

526	1540*	SX	Coleraine

SECTION 4—DISTANCE TABLES

This section contains details of distances along all IR and NIR routes both passenger and freight, together with details of permanent speed restrictions and their locations. The information is arranged in tabular form as follows:

1st Column—Place. Open passenger stations are shown in CAPITALS.

2nd Column—Milepost Distance shown in miles and chains.

3rd Column—Distance along the route from the station shown at the head of the table (shown in miles).

4th Column—Details of locations of permanent speed restrictions. U relates to the Up direction only and D relates to the down direction only. Locations are given in relation to the milepost mileages as shown in the 1st column.

5th Column—Cross references with other tables are given at stations and junctions where appropriate.

INDEX TO TABLES

TABLE 1 - Dublin Heuston–Cobh

Line Maximum Speed 90 mph Dublin Heuston to Cork.
    50 mph Cork to Cobh.

Double line throughout.

DUBLIN HEUSTON	0:00	0.00	40	D 0–1	
			10	U 0½–0	
			60	U 3–0½	
Islandbridge Junction	0:53	0.66	70	D 1–3	Table 32
Inchicore	1:60	1.75			
Lucan South	6:33	6.34			
Hazelhatch	10:00	10.00			
Sallins	17:75	17.94			
Caragh	20:73	20.91			
DROICHEAD NUA	25:40	25.50			
CURRAGH	27:40	27.50	70	U 27½–30½	
			70	D 27½–30¼	
KILDARE	30:00	30.00	80	U 32¾–30½	Table 3
Cherryville Junction	32:36	32.45			Table 3
Monasterevan	36:34	36.43			
PORTARLINGTON	41:58	41.73	60	Through Station	Table 8
			80	U 51–47¼	
Straboe	47:75	47.94			
PORTLAOISE	50:72	50.90			Table 26
Clonkeen	53:37	53.46			
Cuddagh	61:50	61.63			
BALLYBROPHY	66:59	66.74	70	Through Station	Table 6
			80	69–69¼	
			80	72¼–72¾	
Lisduff	72:34	72.43			
TEMPLEMORE	78:67	78.84			
THURLES	86:40	86.50			
Thurles Sugar Factory	87:20	87.25	70	87¼–87¾	
			80	87¾–89¾	
			80	94–94¼	
Goold's Cross	95:09	95.11			
Dundrum	99:39	99.49	80	D 102½–103¾	
			80	U 105–103¾	
Kyle Crossing	106:23	106.29	60	106¼–108¼	Table 2
LIMERICK JUNCTION	107:00	107.00	15	On Platform Roads	Table 5
			75	D 108¼–120	
			75	U 117¾–108¼	
Knocklong	117.04	117.05	75	U 129–124	
Killmallock	124:09	124.11	75	D 126–129	
			80	129–131¼	
RATHLUIRC	129:16	129.20	85	131¼–138½	
Buttevant	137:16	137.20	80	D 138½–140¾	
			80	U 139½–138½	
			75	U 144¼–139½	
			80	D 143–143¾	
MALLOW	144:37	144.46	60	143¾–145¼	Table 7
Killarney Junction	145:18	145.23	65	D 145¼–147	Table 7
Mourne Abbey	148:18	148.23	65	U 163¾–150¼	
			65	D 150¾–151½	
			60	D 151½–154½	
Rathduff	154:24	154.30	75	D 154½–155¼	
			65	D 158½–162	
Blarney	159:28	159.35			
Rathpeacon	161:31	161.39	60	D 162–163½	
Kilbarry	163:16	163.20	50	D 163½–164¼	
			40	U 164¼–163¾	
			30	164¼–165:10	
CORK	165:40	165.50	15	Through Station	

Tivoli	166:60	166.75		
LITTLE ISLAND	169:70	169.88		
COBH JUNCTION	171:17	171.21		Table 23
FOTA	172:41	172.51		
CARRIGALOE	174:25	174.31		
RUSHBROOKE	175:60	175.75		
COBH	176:60	176.75		

Speed restriction on the up loop between Dublin Heuston and Islandbridge Junction is 30 mph.

TABLE 2 Kyle Crossing–Milltown Crossing

Line Maximum Speed 20 mph. Single line throughout.

THURLES	86:40	0.00		
Kyle Crossing	106:23	19.79		Table 1
Milltown Crossing	106:70	20.38		
(Mileage Change)	21:33			Table 4
LIMERICK	0:00	41.79		

TABLE 3 Kildare–Waterford

Line Maximum Speed 70 mph Kildare to Milepost 38¼ (beyond Bennetsbridge).
60 mph Milepost 38¼ (beyond Bennetsbridge) to Waterford.

Single line throughout.

KILDARE	30:00	0.00			Table 1
Cherryville Junction	32:36	2.45	20	Through Junction	Table 1
Kilberry	40:70	10.88			
ATHY	44:64	14.80			
Mageney	51:00	21.00	60	52½–55¾	
CARLOW	55:68	25.85	30	Through Station	
Milford	60:09	30.11			
MUINE BHEAG	65:78	35.98	60	67–69¾	
Jordanstown	70:35	40.44	60	76¼–78½	
Lavistown Junction	78:40	48.50	60	Through Junction	
KILKENNY	80:66	50.83			
(Mileage Change)	28:35	50.83			
Lavistown Junction	30:61	53.16	50	Through Junction	
Bennetsbridge	34:15	56.58	40	38½–39½	
THOMASTOWN	39:04	61.44	50	41–41½	
Ballyhale	43:23	65.68	50	50¾–52¼	
Mullinavat	51:45	73.96			
Kilmacow	54:45	76.96			
Dunkitt	56:60	79.14			
Waterford West	57:56	80.09			
(Mileage Change)	75:20	80.09	30	75¼–76	Tables 4 & 25
WATERFORD	76:00	80.84			

TABLE 4 Limerick–Rosslare Harbour Pier

Line Maximum Speed 60 mph Limerick to Keane's Points.
50 mph Keane's Points to Rosslare Harbour.

Single line Killonan Junction to Waterford West Junction.

LIMERICK	0:00	0.00	15	U 0¼–0	
			25	D 0–0¼	
Limerick Check	0:45	0.56			Tables 20 & 21
Ennis Junction	0:70	0.88	40	2¾–3¼	Table 20
Killonan Junction	4:20	4.25	40	Through Junction	Table 6
Boher	7:50	7.63			
Dromkeen	11:46	11.58			
Cross	15:41	15.51			

Milltown Crossing	21:33	21.41			Table 2
Keane's Points	21:56	21.70			Table 5
TIPPERARY	24:63	24.79			
Cappagh	33:03	33.04	40	36–38¼	
CAHIR	38:26	38.33			
Nicholastown	43:19	43.24	40	46½–48¼	
CLONMEL	49:20	49.25			
Kilsheelan	55:33	55.41			
CARRICK ON SUIR	63:06	63.08			
Fiddown	67:28	67.35			
Grange	70:03	70.04			
Dunkitt	75:44	75.55	30	Over Viaduct	
Waterford West	76:40	76.50			Tables 3 & 25
(Mileage Change)	75:20	76.50	30	75¼–76½	
WATERFORD	76:00	77.25			
Abbey Junction	76.20	77.50	10	Through Junction	
			45	76½–77½	Table 24
			40	80¾–81:30	
Barrow Bridge	81:40	82.75	30	Over Barrow Bridge	
CAMPILE	84:48	85.85	40	Through Station	
BALLYCULLANE	89:25	90.56	40	Through Station	
WELLINGTON BRIDGE	93:27	94.59			
Duncormick	98:02	99.28			
BRIDGETOWN	103:72	105.15	40	Through Station	
Killinick	107:54	108.93	40	Through Station	
ROSSLARE STRAND	110:66	112.08	40	Through Station	Table 14
ROSSLARE HBR MAINLAND	114:00	115.25	15	113½–113¾	
(New Station)			5	113¾–114¼	
Rosslare Harbour Pier	114:20	115.50			

TABLE 5 Keane's Points–Limerick Junction.

Line Maximum Speed 15 mph. Single line throughout.

LIMERICK	0:00	0.00	
Keane's Points	21:56	21.70	Table 4
LIMERICK JUNCTION	21:78	21.98	
(Mileage Change)	107:00		Table 1

TABLE 6 Ballybrophy–Limerick.

Line Maximum Speed 60 mph. Single line Ballybrophy to Killonan Junction.

BALLYBROPHY	66:59				Table 1
(Mileage Change)	0:00	0.00	40	0–0½	
			40	9½–11	
ROSCREA	10:04	10.05			
CLOUGHJORDAN	20:00	20.00			
NENAGH	29:33	29.41	40	Through Station	
Silvermines Junction	35:19	35.24	50	35½–41	Table 22
BIRDHILL	42:36	42.45	40	Through Station	
CASTLECONNELL	47:03	47.04	40	48¼–50	
			50	51¾–52¾	
Killonan Junction	52:48	52.60			
(Mileage Change)	4:20	52.60	40	3¼–2¾	Table 4
			25	D 0–0¼	
Ennis Junction	0:70	55.98			
Limerick Check	0:45	56.29	15	U 0¼–0	
LIMERICK	0:00	56.85			

TABLE 7 Mallow–Tralee.

Line Maximum Speed 60 mph. Single Line Killarney Junction to Tralee.

MALLOW	144:37	0.00			Table 1
Killarney Junction	145:18	0.76			Table 1
(Mileage Change)	0:00	0.76	40	Through Junction	
Beet Factory Siding	1:24	2.06			
Lombardstown	5:40	6.26			
BANTEER	10:60	11.51	25	D Through Station	
			40	U Through Station	
MILLSTREET	19:00	19.76	40	Through Station	
RATHMORE	25:37	26.23	25	Through Station	
KILLARNEY	39:67	40.60			
FARRANFORE	50:44	51.31	40	Through Station	
			40	51¼–51½	
Gortatlea	54:28	55.11	50	55–56½	
TRALEE	61:35	62.20			

TABLE 8 Portarlington–Galway.

Line Maximum Speed 70 mph. Single line Portarlington Junction to Galway.

PORTARLINGTON	41:58	0.00			Table 1
Portarlington Junction	41:60	0.03	10	Through Junction	
			30	41¾–42	
Bord Na Mona Bridge	45:50	3.90			
Geashill	50:24	8.58	50	Through Station	
			40	57½–58	
TULLAMORE	57:71	16.16	60	62¾–63¼	
CLARA	65:00	23.28	40	Through Station	
			50	69¼–69½	
			50	70¾–71¾	
Clonydonnin	73:00	31.28			
ATHLONE	80:40	38.78	20	80½–80:65	
Shannon Bridge	80:65	39.09	20	Over Bridge	
Athlone Midland	81:00	39.28			Table 11
(Mileage Change)	78:05	39.28			Table 13
Athlone West Junction	78:24	39.51			
Carrowduff	84:71	46.10	50	85¼–87¼	
			50	91:30–91¾	
BALLINASLOE	91:53	52.87	50	101¼–102¾	
WOODLAWN	101:40	62.71	50	105½–105¾	
ATTYMON JUNCTION	107:15	68.40	50	Through Junction	
			50	108–108½	
			50	110¾–111¼	
ATHENRY	113:36	74.66	40	Through Loop Xover	Table 20
Oranmore Siding	121:32	82.61	50	125¼–126	
GALWAY	126:53	87.87	30	126–126¼	

TABLE 9 Dublin Connolly–Sligo.

Line Maximum Speed 30 mph Dublin Connolly to Liffey Junction.
70 mph Liffey Junction to Sligo.

Single line Clonsilla to Sligo.

DUBLIN CONNOLLY	0:00	0.00			Tables 14 & 15
(Mileage Change)	1:00	0.00			Tables 10 & 14
West Road	1:24	0.30			
North Strand Junction	1:44	0.55			
(Mileage Change)	4:18	0.55			Table 32
Glasnevin Junction	2:55	2.09	20	Through Junction	Table 32
(Mileage Change)	0:58	2.09			Table 10

84

Station	Time	Mileage	Speed	Notes
Liffey Junction	1:36	2.81	20	Through Junction
(Mileage Change)	1:33	2.81		Table 10
ASHTOWN	3:08	4.50	50	3–3¾
			60	4¼–4½
			60	5¼–6
CLONSILLA	7:08	8.50	40	D Over Jn at W End
			60	7½–8
			50	8¾–9¼
			40	10¾–11¾
LEIXLIP	11:20	12.15	60	11¾–12½
MAYNOOTH	14:72	16.30	50	Through Station
			50	15–15¼
			60	18½–19¼
Kilcock	19:12	20.55	60	22½–24¾
ENFIELD	26:40	27.90	60	Through Station
			50	28¾–29¾
			60	29¾–30½
			50	30½–31¼
			60	31¼–32¾
			50	32¾–33¾
			60	33¾–34½
Hill of Down	35:55	37.09		
Killucan	41:60	43.15	60	43–44
			50	45¾–46¼
			50	48–50¼
MULLINGAR	50:17	51.61	20	Through Station Table 13
Multyfarnham	57:63	59.19	50	65–65¾
MOSTRIM	67:42	68.92	25	U W End Turnout
LONGFORD	76:22	77.67	50	76:30–77:30
			50	82½–83¼
			50	85–86
DROMOD	87:22	88.67	40	Through Station
Shannon Bridge	92:00	93.40	40	Over Bridge
			50	95¾–96¾
			50	97¼–97¾
CARRICK ON SHANNON	97:62	99.17	20	97¾–97:70
			50	97:70–98:30
BOYLE	106:28	107.75	60	107–109¼
			60	112:50–113¼
			50	118½–119
BALLYMOTE	120:06	121.47	40	Through Station
COLLOONEY	127:56	129.10		
Collooney Junction	128:03	129.44	60	129¼–130¼
SLIGO	134:16	135.40		Table 27

TABLE 10 Dublin Connolly–Liffey Junction

Line Maximum Speed 30 mph. Double line throughout.

Station	Time	Mileage	Speed	Notes
DUBLIN CONNOLLY	1:00	0.00		Tables 9 & 14
(Mileage Change)	2:46	0.00	10	02:46–02:24
Newcomen Junction	2:24	0.28		Table 34
Glasnevin Junction	0:58	1.85		Table 9
Liffey Junction	1:36	2.57	20	Through Junction
(Mileage Change)	1:33	2.57		Table 9
ASHTOWN	3:08	4.22		

TABLE 11 Athlone–Westport

Line Maximum Speed 70 mph. Single line throughout.

ATHLONE	80:40	0.00				
Shannon Bridge	80:65	0.31	20	Over Bridge		
Athlone Midland	81:00	0.50				Table 13
(Mileage Change)	78:05	0.50				Table 9
Athlone West Junction	78:24	0.74	20	78¼–78:70		
			50	81–84¾		
Lecarrow	88:20	10.69				
Knockcroghery	90:00	12.44	50	93½–94¾		
			40	95:70–96¼		
ROSCOMMON	96:20	18.69	20	U Through Loop		
			30	96¼–96¾		
			50	103¾–104½		
Ballymoe	107:55	30.13	45	112¼–112½		
CASTLEREA	112:60	35.19	50	116¾–117		
Ballinlough	118:60	41.19				
BALLYHAUNIS	124:12	46.59	20	Through Turnouts		
			30	Through Station		
			30	134½–134:70		
CLAREMORRIS	135:00	57.44	25	Over E. End Xover	Table 20	
			50	135¼–135½		
Balla	142:35	64.88				
MANULLA JUNCTION	145:71	68.33	50	146¼–146¾	Table 12	
			30	149:70–150:50		
CASTLEBAR	150:10	72.56	50	151½–157¾		
Islandeady	155:39	77.93	50	159–161		
WESTPORT	161:11	83.58				

TABLE 12 Manulla Junction–Ballina

Line Maximum Speed 50 mph Manulla Junction to Ballina. Single line throughout.

MANULLA JUNCTION	145:71	0.00	20	145:71–146½	Table 11
Ballyvary	150:30	4.49			
River Moy Bridge	156:00	10.11	10	Over Bridge	
FOXFORD	157:14	11.29			
BALLINA	166:44	20.66			

TABLE 13 Mullingar–Athlone Midland.

Line Maximum Speed 40 mph. Single line throughout.

MULLINGAR	50:17	0.00			Table 9
Castletown	58:22	8.07			
Moate	68:33	18.20			
Shannon Bridge	77:70	27.67	20	Over Bridge	
Athlone Midland	78:05	27.85			Tables 8 & 11

TABLE 14 Dublin Connolly–Rosslare Harbour Pier

Line Maximum Speed   60 mph Dublin Connolly to Rosslare Strand
                     50 mph Rosslare Strand to Rosslare Harbour

Double line to Bray.

DUBLIN CONNOLLY	0:00	0.00	20	Through Station	Tables 9 & 15
(Mileage Change)	1:00	0.00	30	1–0	Tables 9 & 10
TARA STREET	0:20	0.75			
DUBLIN PEARSE	0:00	1.00	30	Through Station	
LANSDOWNE ROAD	1:07	2.09			
SANDYMOUNT	1:52	2.65			
SYDNEY PARADE	2:20	3.25			

BOOTERSTOWN	3:20	4.25		
BLACKROCK	4:07	5.09		
MONKSTOWN & SEAPOINT	4:60	5.75		
SALTHILL	5:26	6.33	30	5¾–7¼
DUN LAOGHAIRE	6:00	7.00		
SANDYCOVE	6:58	7.73		
GLENAGEARY	7:20	8.25		
DALKEY	8:05	9.06	30	8¼–9½
KILLINEY	9:74	10.93		
SHANKILL	11:00	12.00		
Shanganagh Junction	11:77	12.96		
(Mileage Change)	10:42	12.96		
BRAY	12:20	14.69	40	Xover at N End
			20	13¼–15
			40	15–15½
GREYSTONES	17:05	19.50	50	18–23
KILCOOLE	19:66	22.26		
Newcastle	22:38	24.91		
Wicklow Junction	27:60	30.19	20	27¾–28¼
WICKLOW	28:20	30.69		
Ballymanus	32:54	35.11		
RATHDRUM	37:24	39.74	50	38–48
Avoca	42:66	45.26		
Shelton Abbey	46:68	49.29		
ARKLOW	49:00	51.44		
Inch	53:38	55.91	50	58–58½
GOREY	59:33	61.85	40	Through Station
Ferns	69:71	72.33	50	76¼–77½
ENNISCORTHY	77:40	79.94	30	77¾–78¼
			40	78¼–78½
			50	83½–84
			50	86–86½
Killurin	86:16	88.64	40	86½–87
			50	87–90
			30	90–90½
WEXFORD	93:00	95.44	5	93–5:25
(Mileage Change)	6:20	95.44		
Wexford South	5:25	96.38	40	5¼–5
ROSSLARE STRAND	0:00	101.69	40	Through Station	Table 4
(Mileage Change)	110:66	101.69		
ROSSLARE HBR MAINLAND	114:00	104.87	15	113½–113¾
(New Station)			5	113¾–114
Rosslare Harbour Pier	114:20	105.14		

TABLE 15 Dublin Connolly–Bangor

Line Maximum Speed 70 mph. Double line throughout.

DUBLIN CONNOLLY	0:00	0.00	20	From Sub. Plats	Tables 9 & 14
			25	U 0¾–0	
East Wall Junction	0:57	0.71			Table 33
KILLESTER	2:31	2.39			
HARMONSTOWN	3:00	3.00			
RAHENY	3:57	3.71			
KILBARRACK	4:40	4.50			
HOWTH JUNCTION	4:64	4.80			Table 16
PORTMARNOCK	6:56	6.70			

MALAHIDE	9:00	9.00			
DONABATE	11:35	11.44			
RUSH & LUSK	13:74	13.93			
SKERRIES	17:77	17.96			
BALBRIGGAN	21:60	21.75			
GORMANSTON	24:00	24.00			
MOSNEY	25:63	25.79			
LAYTOWN	27:13	27.16			
DROGHEDA	31:60	31.75	15	Through Station	Table 28
Boyne Viaduct	32:00	32.00	15	Over Viaduct	
Cement Branch Junction	32:48	32.60			Table 30
Kellystown	37:24	37.30			
Dunleer	41:56	41.70			
Dromin Junction	43:51	43.64			
Castlebellingham	47:16	47.20			
Dundalk South Junction	53:40	53.50			Table 31
DUNDALK	54:30	54.38	40	Through Station	
Border Post (IR/NIR)	59:48	59.80			
Meigh	63:09	63.11			
NEWRY	69:20	69.25			
Knockarney	73:41	73.51	40	76½–77	
POYNTZPASS	76:73	76.91			
Acton	78:05	78.06	50	79–79½	
SCARVA	79:47	79.59			
Adams	84:50	84.63	15	87–87½	
PORTADOWN	87:16	87.20			
Boilie	90:51	90.64			
LURGAN	92:43	92.54			
Kilmore	94:67	94.84			
MOIRA	98:03	98.04			
Damhead	100:00	100.00			
Knockmore Junction	103:35	103.44			Table 17
KNOCKMORE	104:00	104.00			
LISBURN	105:04	105.05	60	105¼–106¾	Table 17
HILDEN	106:01	106.01			
LAMBEG	106:45	106.56			
DERRIAGHY	107:40	107.50			
DUNMURRY	108:40	108.50			
FINAGHY	109:40	109.50			
BALMORAL	110:24	110.30			
ADELAIDE	111:15	111.19	30	113¾–112¼	
CITY HOSPITAL	112:20	112.25	40	112¼–113	
BOTANIC	112:40	112.50			
BELFAST CENTRAL	113:40	113.50	15	Through Station	
		0.00	30	113¼–114	
			40	114–114¼	
BRIDGE END	114:20	0.75			
Victoria Park	115:00	1.50			
SYDENHAM	115:46	2.08	50	118¼–118½	
HOLYWOOD	118:33	4.91			
MARINO	119:03	5.54			
CULTRA	119:59	6.24			
Craigavad	120:21	6.76	60	120¾–121¼	
SEAHILL	121:33	7.91			
HELEN'S BAY	122:56	9.20	50	123–123½	
CRAWFORDSBURN	123:39	9.99			
CARNALEA	124:16	10.70			
BANGOR WEST	124:76	11.45	50	125–125:76	
BANGOR	125:76	12.45			

Speed Restriction on the 3rd road at Dundalk Station is 20 mph.

TABLE 16 Howth Junction–Howth

Line Maximum Speed 50 mph. Double line throughout.

HOWTH JUNCTION	4:64	0.00	20	Through Junction	Table 15
(Mileage Change)	0:00	0.00			
BAYSIDE	1:00	1.00			
SUTTON	1:60	1.75			
HOWTH	3:34	3.43			

TABLE 17 Lisburn–Londonderry

Line Maximum Speed 70 mph. Double line Antrim to Ballymena only.

LISBURN	105:04	0.00	15	105:04–104¾	Table 15
Knockmore Junction	103:35	1.61			Table 15
(Mileage Change)	0:00	1.61	50	0–0¼	
BALLINDERRY	5:26	6.94	40	8½–8¾	
GLENAVY	8:50	10.24			
CRUMLIN	10:72	12.51	30	11–11½	
Aldergrove	13:16	14.81	40	18¼–18½	
ANTRIM	18:40	20.11	15	Through Station	
(Mileage Change)	21:60	20.11	60	D 21¾–32¾	Table 35
Skegeneagh	25:31	23.75			
Kellswater	28:70	26.24			
Slaght	31:22	29.64	40	32¾–33¾	
BALLYMENA	33:40	31.86			
CULLYBACKEY	36:38	34.84			
Glarryford	41:17	39.57			
Killagan	43:33	41.77			
Dunloy	46:12	44.51			
Ballyboyland	50:33	48.77	40	53½–53¾	
BALLYMONEY	53:36	51.81			
Macfin	57:05	55.42	40	61½–62¾	
COLERAINE	61.60	60.11			Table 18
Grangemore	65:12	63.51			
CASTLEROCK	67.40	65.86	40	Through Station	
Magilligan	71:76	70.31			
BELLARENA	74.76	73.31	50	79½–79¾	
Limavady Junction	79:55	78.05			
Ballykelly	81:51	80.00			
Eglinton	87:58	86.09			
Lisahally	90:68	89.21	40	94¾–95¼	
LONDONDERRY	95:20	93.61			

TABLE 18 Coleraine–Portrush

Line Maximum Speed 50 mph. Single line throughout.

COLERAINE	61:60	0.00	40	Over Junction	Table 17
UNIVERSITY	63:00	1.25			
Cromore	65:00	3.25			
DHU VARREN	67:20	5.50			
PORTRUSH	67:60	6.00			

TABLE 19 Belfast York Road–Larne Harbour

Line Maximum Speed 70 mph. Double line Belfast York Road to Whitehead.

BELFAST YORK ROAD	0:00	00.00	60	0–3½	
Fortwilliam	1:60	1.75	30	3½–3¾	
			60	3¾–4½	
WHITEABBEY	4:24	4.30	50	D 4½–5½	
Bleach Green Junction	4:56	4.70	50	Over Junction	Table 35
JORDANSTOWN	5:28	5.35			

GREENISLAND	6:56	6.70		
TROOPERSLANE	7:72	7.90		
CLIPPERSTOWN	9:20	9.25		
CARRICKFERGUS	9:43	9.54	50	D Through Station
DOWNSHIRE	10:38	10.48	50	D 13–14½
			50	U 14¾–13
Whitehead Tunnel	14:00	14.00		
WHITEHEAD	14:55	14.69	30	D Through Station
BALLYCARRY	16:40	16.50		
Magheramorne Loop	19:39	19.49	50	19½–20
MAGHERAMORNE	19:60	19.75		
GLYNN	21:48	21.60	40	23–24:17
LARNE TOWN	23:20	23.25	30	Single to D Xover
LARNE HARBOUR	24:17	24.21		

TABLE 20 Claremorris–Foynes

Line Maximum Speed 40 mph Claremorris to Ennis.
50 mph Ennis to Limerick Check.
30 mph Limerick Check to Foynes.

Single line throughout.

CLAREMORRIS	135:00	0.00			Tables 11 & 12
(Mileage Change)	17:00	0.00	25	16½–14	
Ballandine	12:44	4.45			
Milltown	8:49	8.61	25	8½–7	
Castlegrove	4:37	12.54	25	Over L Crossing	
Tuam Sugar Factory	1:50	15.38			
Tuam	0:00	17.00			
(Mileage Change)	76:15	17.00	30	75–72	
			25	70–69	
Ballyglunin	69:76	23.24	25	66¾–65¼	
			25	61½–61¼	
ATHENRY	59:69	33.33	25	56:10–54:70	Table 8
Craughwell	55:13	38.03	25	53–52	
Ardrahan	49:06	44.11			
Gort	42:25	50.88			
Crusheen	32:37	60.73	25	32:30–31	
Upper Fergus Bridge	25:30	67.81	20	Over Bridge	
			25	25:30–24½	
Ennis	24:60	68.44	40	23½–23¼	
Clarecastle Siding	23:00	70.19			
Ballycar	16:58	76.46	40	12½–12	
			40	10½–9¾	
Cratloe	9:60	83.44			
Meelick	6:32	86.79			
Long Pavement	3:70	89.31	30	Over L Crossing	
Shannon Bridge	3:49	89.58			
Canal Bridge	2:40	90.69	15	Over Bridge	
			25	1¾–0¾	
Ennis Junction	0:70	92.31			Table 4
Limerick Check	0:45	92.63			Tables 4 & 21
(Mileage Change)	0:45	0.00			
Foynes Junction	1:00	0.44			
Patrickswell	7:26	6.76			
Adare	11:04	10.49			
Ballingrane Junction	17:27	16.78			
Askeaton	20:70	20.31			
Robertstown Viaduct	25:00	24.44	15	Over Viaduct	
Foynes	26:65	26.25			

90

TABLE 21 Limerick Check–Castlemungret

Line Maximum Speed 20 mph. Single line throughout.

Limerick Check	0:45			Tables 4 & 20
(Mileage Change)	0:00	0.00		
Rosbrien Curve			15 Through Curve	
Castlemungret	4:45	4.56		

TABLE 22 Silvermines Junction–Silvermines

Line Maximum Speed 10 mph (Down), 5 mph (Up). Single line throughout.

Silvermines Junction	35:19	0.00	Table 6
(Mileage Change)	0:00	0.00	
Silvermines	1:20	1.25	

TABLE 23 Cobh Junction–Youghal

Line Maximum Speed 20 mph. Single line throughout.

COBH JUNCTION	171:17	0.00			Table 1
(Mileage Change)	0:00	0.00	5	at 5¾	
Midleton	6:18	6.23			
Mogeely	11:38	11.48			
Killeagh	14:15	14.19			
Youghal	20:63	20.79			

TABLE 24 Abbey Junction–New Ross

Line Maximum Speed 20 mph. Single line throughout.

Abbey Junction	76:20	0.00			Table 4
(Mileage Change)	115:40	0.00	10	Through Junction	
Glenmore	108:00	7.50			
Main Road Level Xing	102:60	12.75	5	102¾–102½	
Staffords Level Xing	102:40	13.00			
New Ross	102:00	13.50			

TABLE 25 Ballinacourty–Waterford

Line Maximum Speed 20 mph. Single line throughout.

Ballinacourty	49:00	0.00	
Waterford West	75:20	26.25	
WATERFORD	76:00	27.00	Tables 3 & 4

TABLE 26 Portlaoise–Coolnamona

Line Maximum Speed 25 mph. Single line throughout.

PORTLAOISE	50:72	0.00	Table 1
(Mileage Change)	0:00	0.00	
Coolnamona	2:60	2.75	

TABLE 27 Sligo–Sligo Quay

Line Maximum Speed 10 mph. Single line throughout.

SLIGO	134:16	0.00	Table 9
(Mileage Change)	0:00	0.00	
Sligo Quay	0:20	0.25	

TABLE 28 Drogheda–Kingscourt

Line Maximum Speed   40 mph Drogheda to Navan.
                               25 mph Navan to Kingscourt.

Single line throughout.

DROGHEDA	31:60	0.00			Table 15
(Mileage Change)	0:00	0.00			
Platin Cement Factory	2:60	2.75	25	2¾–3¼	
Lougher	8:40	8.50			
Navan	16:75	16.94			
Tara Mines Junction	17:20	17.25			Table 29
(Mileage Change)	30:42	17.25			
Castletown	39:70	26.60			
Kingscourt	50:45	37.29			

TABLE 29 Tara Mines Junction–Tara Mines

Line Maximum Speed 25 mph. Single line throughout.

Tara Mines Junction	17:20	0.00	Table 28
Tara Mines	17:40	0.25	

Table 30–Cement Branch Junction to Boyne Road Cement Siding.

Line Maximum Speed 15 mph. Single line throughout.

Cement Branch Junction	32:48	0.00	Table 15
(Mileage Change)	0:00	0.00	
Boyne Road Cement Siding	0:60	0.75	

TABLE 31 Dundalk South Junction–Barrack Street Goods.

Line Maximum Speed 25 mph. Single line throughout.

Dundalk South Junction	53:40	0.00	Table 15
(Mileage Change)	0:00	0.00	
Barrack Street Goods	1:40	01.50	

TABLE 32 Islandbridge Junction–Alexandra Road

Line Maximum Speed 30 mph. Double line throughout.

Islandbridge Junction	0:53	0.00			Table 1
(Mileage Change)	0:00	0.00	20	Through Junction	
Cabra	1:68	1.85			
Glasnevin Junction	2:55	2.69			Table 9
North Strand Junction	4:18	4.23			Table 9
Church Road Junction	4:51	4.64	20	Through Junction	Table 33
			20	04:51–5	
Granaries	5:00	5.00	20	5–6¼	
Alexandra Road	6:20	6.25			

TABLE 33 Church Road Junction–East Wall Junction.

Line Maximum Speed 20 mph.

Church Road Junction	4:51	0.00	Table 32
(Mileage Change)	0:00	0.00	
East Wall Junction	0:40	0.50	
(Mileage Change)	0:57	0.50	Table 15

TABLE 34 Newcomen Junction–North Wall Container Terminal.

Line Maximum Speed 20 mph.

Newcomen Junction	2:24	0.00	Table 10
North Wall Container Terminal	1:48	0.70	

TABLE 35 Bleach Green Junction–Antrim

Line Maximum Speed 60 mph. Single line Monkstown to Antrim.

Bleach Green Junction	4:56	0.00			Table 19
Monkstown	6:05	1.36			
(Mileage Change)	8:46	1.36	30	Single to Up Xover	
Mossley	9:41	2.30			
Kingsmoss No.1	11:15	3.98			
Kingsmoss No.2	11:30	4.16			
Kingsbog	11:60	4.54			
Ballymartin	14:67	7.63			
Templepatrick	16:26	9.11			
Kilmakee	17:38	10.26			
Muckamore	19:68	12.64	30	$21\frac{1}{4}$–$21\frac{1}{2}$	
ANTRIM	21:60	14.54	15	Single to D Xover	Table 17

▲ **A Multi-Engined dmu headed by power car 27 enters Lisburn with the 1505 from Bangor on 29th August 1977.**

Jonathan Allen

SECTION 5—CLOSED PASSENGER RAILWAYS OF IRELAND.

Over the years, the rail network in both the Irish Republic and Northern Ireland has contracted sharply, especially during the early part of the 1960's, as more and more services became uneconomic to run. The rash of closures in the early 1960's was mainly due to the recommendations contained in the Beddy Commission Report of 1957 on the rail network, which was furthered under the terms of the 1958 Transport Act which allowed CIE greater commercial freedom. This act repealed some of the old restrictions imposed by previous legislation and allowed CIE to close down certain uneconomic services. This section gives an indication as to when a great deal of routes and services were closed, but is not intended to be exhaustive.

LINES CLOSED AND LIFTED

Section	Date closed completely	Company at closure
Keady–Castleblaney	10.08.24	GNR (I)
Listowel–Ballybunion	14.10.24	L & B
Blessington–Poulaphouca	30.09.27	D & B
Kinsale Junction–Kinsale	01.09.31	GSR
Monkstown–Crosshaven	31.05.32	GSR
Cork–Monkstown	10.09.32	GSR
Dublin–Blessington	31.12.32	D & B
Ballyclare–Doagh	. .33	NCC
Markethill–Armagh	.02.33	GNR (I)
Castlederg–Victoria Bridge	17.04.33	C & VB
Ballina–Killala	01.07.34	GSR
Muskerry, Coachford, Blarney & Donaghmore branches	31.12.34	GSR
Clifden–Galway	29.04.35	GSR
Buncrana–Carndonagh	02.12.35	L & LSR
Rathkenny–Retreat	10.04.37	NCC
Achill–Westport	01.10.37	GSR
Castlegregory–Castlegregory Jn.	17.04.39	GSR
Ballymena–Rathkenny	. .40	NCC
Gweedore–Burtonport	01.06.40	L & LSR
Maguiresbridge–Tynan	31.12.41	CVR
Ballyboley–Ballymena	. .42	NCC
Killaloe–Birdhill	24.04.44	GSR
Shillelagh–Woodenbridge Jn.	24.04.44	GSR
Killashandra–Crossdoney	27.01.47	CIE
Clara–Streamstown	27.01.47	CIE
Mitchelstown–Fermoy	27.01.47	CIE
Schull–Skibbereen	27.01.47	CIE
Dingle–Tralee	10.03.47	CIE
Letterkenny–Gweedore	01.06.47	L & LSR
Glenties–Stranorlar	31.12.47	CDJ
Newry–Bessbrook	10.01.48	B & N
Giant's Causeway–Portstewart	. .49	GC
Newcastle–Comber	15.01.50	UTA
Ballynahinch–Ballynahinch Jn.	15.01.50	UTA
Downpatrick–Ardglass	15.01.50	UTA
Ballymacarrett Jn.–Donaghdee	15.01.50	UTA
Larne–Ballyclare Jn.	03.07.50	UTA
Ballycastle–Ballymoney	03.07.50	UTA
Dundalk–Greenore	31.12.51	DN & G
Newry–Greenore	31.12.51	DN & G
Buncrana–Londonderry	10.08.53	L & LS
Letterkenny–Tooban Jn.	10.08.53	L & LS
Macroom–Cork	01.01.54	CIE
Athboy–Kilmessan	01.01.54	CIE

Cashel–Goolds Cross	.09.54	CIE
Strabane–Londonderry	31.12.54	CDJ
Magherafelt–Cookstown	01.05.55	UTA
Dungiven–Limavady Junction	01.05.55	UTA
Newcastle–Castlewellan	01.05.55	UTA
Scarva–Castlewellan	01.05.55	GNR (I)
Goraghwood–Markethill	01.05.55	GNR (I)
Banbridge–Knockmore Junction	29.04.56	GNR (I)
Kilrea–Macfin	. .57	GNR (I)
Draperstown–Magherafelt	. .57	GNR (I)
Armagh–Keady	01.10.57	GNR (I)
Portadown–Monaghan	01.10.57	GNR (I)
Clones–Omagh	01.10.57	GNR (I)
Bundoran–Bundoran Jn.	01.10.57	GNR (I)
Collooney–Enniskillen	01.10.57	SLNCR
Dublin (Harcourt Street)–Shanganagh Junction	01.01.59	CIE
Tullow–Sallins	15.03.59	CIE
Belturbet–Dromod	01.04.59	CIE
Ballinamore–Arigna	01.04.59	CIE
Belturbet–Ballyhaise	01.04.59	CIE
Cookstown Jn.–Kilrea	01.10.59	UTA
Cookstown–Coalisland	05.10.59	UTA
Stabane–Killybegs	31.12.59	CDJ
Donegal–Ballyshannon	31.12.59	CDJ
Cavan–Inny Junction	01.01.60	CIE
Ballybay–Cootehill	01.01.60	UTA
Clones–Dundalk	01.01.60	UTA
Cavan–Clones	01.01.60	UTA
Inniskeen–Carrickmacross	01.01.60	CIE
Clones–Monaghan	01.01.60	CIE
Ballinrobe–Claremorris	01.01.60	CIE
Kenmare–Headford Junction	01.01.60	CIE
Valentia Harbour–Farranfore	01.02.60	CIE
Tramore–Waterford	31.12.60	CIE
West Clare Railway	01.02.61	CIE
Cork, Bandon & South Coast	01.04.61	CIE
Ballinascarthy–Courtmacsherry	01.04.61	CIE
Portlaoise–Mountmellick	01.01.63	CIE
Roscrea–Birr	01.01.63	CIE
Clara–Banagher	01.01.63	CIE
Portlaoise–Kilkenny	01.01.63	CIE
Kilfree–Ballaghadereen	04.02.63	CIE
Banteer–Newmarket	04.02.63	CIE
Athy–Ballylinan	01.04.63	CIE
Bagenalstown–Palace East	01.04.63	CIE
Enfield–Edenderry	01.04.63	CIE
Clonsilla–Navan	01.04.63	CIE
Navan–Oldcastle	01.04.63	CIE
Macmine–New Ross	01.04.63	CIE
Goraghwood–Warrenpoint	04.01.65	UTA
Coalisland–Dungannon	04.01.65	UTA
Londonderry–Portadown	15.02.65	UTA
Mallow–Ballinacourty Jn.	26.03.67	CIE
Patrickswell–Rathluirc	26.03.67	CIE
Thurles–Clonmel	26.03.67	CIE
Limerick Station–Careys Road	02.10.75	CIE
Attymon Jn.–Loughrea	03.11.75	CIE
Dromin Jn.–Ardee	03.11.75	CIE
Wicklow (Morrough)–Wicklow Jn.	01.11.76	CIE
Westport–Westport Quay	. .77	CIE
Gortatlea–Castleisland	10.01.77	CIE
Curragh–Racecourse Platform	07.03.77	CIE
Dun Laoghaire Carlisle Pier–Pier Jn.	11.10.80	CIE

KEY TO RAILWAY COMPANIES

B & N	-Bessbrook & Newry Railway
C & VB	-Castlederg & Victoria Bridge Railway
CDJ	-County Donegal Joint Railway
CIE	-Coras Iompair Eireann
CVR	-Clogher Valley Railway
D & B	-Dublin & Blessington Railway
DN & G	-Dundalk & Greenore Railway
GC	-Giants Causeway & Portrush Tramway
GNR (I)	-Great Northern Railway (Ireland)
GSR	-Great Southern Railway
L & B	-Listowel & Ballybunion Railway
L & LSR	-Londonderry & Lough Swilly Railway
NCC	-Northern Counties Committee
SLNCR	-Sligo, Leitrim & Northern Counties Railway
UTA	-Ulster Transport Authority

LINES CLOSED BUT STILL IN SITU

Section	Date closed to passenger traffic	Date closed completely	Notes
Tralee–Fenit	31.12.34	05.06.78	Note 1
Claremorris–Collooney Junction	17.06.63	03.11.75	Note 2
Tralee–Abberdorney	04.02.63	05.06.78	Note 3
Abberdorney–Listowel	04.02.63	10.01.77	Note 3
Listowel–Ballingrane Junction	04.02.63	03.11.75	Note 3
Waterford–Ballinacourty	26.03.67	28.07.82	

Most of the above routes remained open for freight traffic and special excursions after the withdrawal of regular passenger services, but all have now been abandoned and are not expected to see any more traffic.

Notes
1. To reopen and be operated by the Great Southern Railway Preservation Society.
2. Severed at Collooney Junction.
3. Lifting in progress.

LINES OPEN FOR FREIGHT TRAFFIC ONLY

Section	Date closed to passenger traffic	Notes
Navan–Kingscourt	27.01.47	
Drogheda–Navan	. .58	*
Cobh Junction–Youghal	04.02.63	
Limerick–Foynes	04.02.63	
Waterford–New Ross	01.04.63	
Limerick–Claremorris	05.04.76	*
Mullingar–Athlone	11.05.87	*
Bleach Green Jn.–Antrim	. .81	*

* denotes still in use for special excursion traffic, albeit on an irregular basis.

Key For Page 97.

*	Passed for main line running.	B & CDR	Belfast & County Down Railway.
GS & WR	Great Southern & Western Railway.	D & SER	Dublin & South Eastern Railway.
SL & NCR	Sligo, Leitrim & Northern Counties Railway.		

SECTION 6–PRESERVED STEAM LOCOS

The following 5ft 3in gauge locomotives are preserved in Ireland:

No.	Class	Wheels	Builder	Date	Owning Co	Notes
Railway Preservation Society of Ireland, Whitehead, Co. Antrim.						
184	J15	0–6–0	GS & WR, Inchicore	1880	GS & WR	* Based at Mullingar.
186	J15	0–6–0	Sharp Stewart, Manchester	1879	GS & WR	* Awaiting overhaul.
4	WT	2–6–4T	LMS, Derby	1947	NCC	*
171	S	4–4–0	Beyer Peacock, Manchester	1913	GNR(I)	' *
27	Z	0–6–4T	Beyer Peacock, Manchester	1949	SL & NCR	Awaiting overhaul.
461	K2	2–6–0	Beyer Peacock, Manchester	1922	D & SER	Being restored.
Belfast Transport Museum, Witham Street, Belfast.						
30	I	4–4–2T	Beyer Peacock, Manchester	1901	B & CDR.	
74	U2	4–4–0	North British, Glasgow	1924	NCC	
85	V	4–4–0	Beyer Peacock, Manchester	1932	GNR(I)	* Based at Whitehead.
93	JT	2–4–2T	GNR(I), Dundalk	1895	GNR(I)	
800	B1A	4–6–0	GSR, Inchicore	1939	GSR.	
Great Southern Railway Preservation Society, Mallow, Co. Cork.						
131	Qs	4–4–0	Neilson Reid, Glasgow	1901	GNR(I)	Being restored.
Westrail, Tuam, Co. Galway.						
90	J30	0–6–0	GS & WR, Inchicore	1875	GS & WR	

Originally an 0–6–4T loco & carriage combined.

Irish Rail, Kent Station, Cork.

No.	Class	Wheels	Builder	Date	Owning Co	Notes
36	?	2–2–2	Bury, Curtis and Kennedy, Liverpool	1846	GS & WR	On static display.

▲ **MED car no. 28 heads a three car set awaiting departure from Belfast Queen's Quay station with a service for Bangor on 10th April 1976. This was the final day of services from this station.**
Jonathan Allen

APPENDIX 1-FORMER DIESEL RAILCARS & MULTIPLE UNITS OF CIE, NIR & CONSTITUENT COMPANIES.

Note: The author recognises that much information is still required to make this section as complete as the rest of the book. If any readers can help with any of the missing information please contact the author at the publishers address for inclusion in future editions.

NCC RAILCARS
DRIVING MOTOR BRAKE COMPOSITE

Built: 1933 by NCC at York Road Works, Belfast.
Engines: Two Leyland 10 litre petrol, each of 125 hp at 2000 rpm.
Transmission: Hydraulic. Two Lysholm Smith torque converters.
Seats: 6F, 55T. **Length:** 57 ft (17.07 m).
Width: 9ft 8 in (2.95 m). **Weight:** 32 tons.
Brakes: Vacuum.

This vehicle was re-engined in 1947 & 1959, details of revised engines not currently available.

Vehicle No.	Month to Traffic	Month Withdrawn	Month Cut Up	Disposal Location
1	01.33	12.65	-	RPSI Depot, Whitehead (P).

Preserved by the Ulster Folk Museum. Currently awaiting restoration.

DRIVING MOTOR BRAKE COMPOSITE

Built: 1934 by NCC at York Road Works, Belfast.
Engines: Two Leyland of 125 hp (93 kW) each.
Transmission: Hydraulic. Two Lysholm Smith torque converters.
Seats: 5F, 75T. **Length:** 60 ft (18.29 m).
Width: 9 ft (2.74 m). **Weight:** 26 tons.
Brakes: Vacuum.

Vehicle No.	Month to Traffic	Month Withdrawn	Month Cut Up	Disposal Location
2	06.34	.57	?	?

DRIVING MOTOR BRAKE COMPOSITE

Built: 1935 (3) or 1938 (4) by NCC at York Road Works, Belfast.
Engines: Two Leyland of 125 hp (93 kW) each.
Transmission: Hydraulic. Two Lysholm Smith torque converters.
Seats: 12F, 60T. **Length:** 62 ft (18.9 m)
Width: 9 ft 6 in (2.9 m) **Weight:** 28 tons.
Brakes: Vacuum.

3 was fitted with front end doors.
Both vehicles were withdrawn following fire damage, that to 4 being on 18.12.69.

Vehicle No.	Month to Traffic	Month Withdrawn	Month Cut Up	Disposal Location
3	.36	.57	?	?
4	.38	12.68	12.69	Belfast York Road.

TRAILER THIRD

Built: 1934 by NCC at York Road Works, Belfast.
Seats: 100.
Width: 9 ft 5 in (2.88 m).
Brakes: Vacuum.

Length: 62 ft (18.9 m).
Weight: 17.5 tons.

Vehicle No.	Month to Traffic	Month Withdrawn	Month Cut Up	Disposal Location
1	.34	?	-	Converted to 544 (qv).
2	.34	?	-	Converted to 545 (qv).

UTA DIESEL RAILCAR
DRIVING MOTOR BRAKE COMPOSITE

Built: 1936 by Metropolitan Cammell, Birmingham as a demonstration unit. Sold to UTA in February 1951, when it was regauged to 5 ft 3 in.
Engine: Ganz of 240 hp (179 kW) at 1250 rpm.
Transmission:
Seats: 18F, 38T.
Width: 8 ft 7 in (2.63 m).
Brakes: Air.

Length: 64 ft (19.51 m).
Weight: 38 tons.

Used in conjunction with MED intermediate trailer 515.

Vehicle No.	Month to Traffic	Month Withdrawn	Month Cut Up	Disposal Location
5	04.51	05.65	05.65	Belfast Maysfield Yard.

UTA DIESEL MECHANICAL MULTIPLE UNITS
DRIVING MOTOR BRAKE COMPOSITE

Built: 1951 by UTA.
Engines: Two AEC 9.6 litre of 125 hp (93 kW) each.
Transmission: Mechanical.
Seats: 8F, 65T.
Width: 9 ft 5 in (9.88 m).
Brakes: Vacuum.

Length: 61 ft 1 in (18.62 m).
Weight: 35 tons.

Converted from J10 class loco hauled coaches 205 & 207 respectively, built 1937–39.
Used in conjunction with MED intermediate trailer 528.
7 was converted to DMBSO seating 79S in March 1958.

Vehicle No.	Month to Traffic	Month Withdrawn	Month Cut Up	Disposal Location
6	08.51	12.68	12.69	Belfast York Road
7	08.51	12.69	12.69	Belfast York Road

Both vehicles were destroyed by fire at Belfast York Road whilst awaiting disposal in December 1969.

UTA MULTI-ENGINED DIESEL MULTIPLE UNITS (MED)
DRIVING MOTOR COMPOSITE (* DRIVING MOTOR BRAKE COMPOSITE)

Built: 1952–53 by UTA.
Engines: Two Leyland EO 600/177 of 125 hp (93 kW) at 1800 rpm.
Transmission: Hydraulic. Two Lysholm Smith torque converters.
Seats: 12F, 55T (* 12F, 36T).   **Length:** 61 ft 1 in (18.62 m).
Width: 9 ft 5 in (2.88 m).   **Weight:** 35.75 tons.
Brakes: Air.

Converted from J10 class loco hauled coaches 206, 201, 207, 202, 204 & 203 respectively, built 1936–39.
Used in conjunction with power cars 14–35 and trailers 501–514 & 515–528 in 3 or 4 (from 1956/7 onwards) car sets.
All were re-engined with Leyland 680 165 hp (123 kW) engines between March and May 1956, and the DMBCO cars were converted at the same time to DMBTO seating 56T.
The hydraulic transmissions were replaced by mechanical with Wilson 4 speed gearboxes between August 1967 and May 1968.

Vehicle No.	Month to Traffic	Month Withdrawn	Month Cut Up	Disposal Location
8*	03.52	02.76	02.78	Magheramorne
9	03.52	06.75	02.78	Magheramorne
10*	03.52	05.79	09.80	Nutts Corner Airport
11	03.52	11.74	05.80	Ballymena
12*	04.53	10.73	?	?
13	04.53	12.74	05.80	Ballymena

10 was transferred to the RPSI reserve fleet on 04.05.79 to be refurbished with BR transmission parts. However, this project was soon abandoned. The bodyshell of this vehicle was then used as a storage shed at Nutts Corner Airport until September 1980.

DRIVING MOTOR BRAKE THIRD (* DRIVING MOTOR BRAKE COMPOSITE, § DRIVING MOTOR COMPOSITE)

Built: 1953–54 by UTA.
Engines: Two Leyland EO 600/177 of 125 hp (93 kW) at 1800 rpm.
Transmission: Hydraulic. Two Lysholm Smith torque converters.
Seats: 56 (* 12F, 36T. § 12F, 55T).   **Length:** 61 ft 1 in (18.62 m).
Width: 9ft 5 in (2.88 m).   **Weight:** 36 tons.
Brakes: Air.

Converted from J4 & J5† class loco hauled coaches 248, 246, 250, 254, 251, 260†, 252, 257†, 253 & 259† respectively, built 1925–30.
Used in conjunction with power cars 8–13 & 24–35 and trailers 501–514 & 515–528 in 3 or 4 (from 1956/7 onwards) car sets.
All were re-engined with Leyland 680 165 hp (123 kW) engines between June and November 1956, and DMCO cars 15 & 19 were converted at the same time to DMSO seating 75S. 17 was similarly converted in September 1958.
The hydraulic transmissions were replaced by mechanical with Wilson 4 speed gearboxes between December 1966 and December 1969.

Vehicle No.	Month to Traffic	Month Withdrawn	Month Cut Up	Disposal Location
14	11.53	02.77	?	?
15§	11.53	02.77	?	?
16	12.53	01.75	05.80	Ballymena
17§	12.53	11.74	?	Crumlin
18	10.53	10.77	?	?
19§	10.53	05.79	09.80	Nutts Corner Airport
20*	01.54	11.77	?	?
21§	01.54	05.79	09.80	Nutts Corner Airport

22	02.54	01.78	?	?
23§	02.54	?	05.80	Ballymena

19 and 21 were transferred to the RPSI reserve fleet on 04.05.79 to be refurbished with BR transmission parts. However, this project was soon abandoned. The bodyshells of these vehicles were then used as storage sheds at Nutts Corner Airport until September 1980.

DRIVING MOTOR THIRD (* DRIVING MOTOR BRAKE COMPOSITE)

Built: 1952–53 by UTA.
Engines: Two Leyland EO 600/177 of 125 hp (93 kW) at 1800 rpm.
Transmission: Hydraulic. Two Lysholm Smith torque converters.
Seats: 85 (* 8F, 46T). **Length:** 61 ft 3 in (18.67 m).
Width: 9 ft 5 in (2.88 m). **Weight:** 36 tons.
Brakes: Air.

The underframes for 24–30 were built by Metropolitan Cammell in 1950.
The underframe for 31 was built by NCC, being spare from nos. 1–4.
Used in conjunction with power cars 8–23 & 32–35 and trailers 501–514 & 515–528 in 3 or 4 (from 1956/7 onwards) car sets.
All were re-engined with Leyland 680 165 hp (123 kW) engines during April and May 1956, and the DMBCO cars were converted at the same time to DMBTO seating 61T. These cars were subsequently reconverted to DMBCO in September 1958, seating 8F, 46S.
The hydraulic transmissions were replaced by mechanical with Wilson 4 speed gearboxes between January 1968 and July 1969.
Extra driving ends were fitted to 24 & 26 in December 1961 and 28 in January 1962 using equipment removed from 505–507.

Vehicle No.	Month to Traffic	Month Withdrawn	Month Cut Up	Disposal Location
24*	08.52	12.76	05.80	Crosshill Quarry, Co. Antrim (A).
25	08.52	?	05.80	Crosshill Quarry, Co. Antrim (A).
26*	10.52	?	05.80	Crosshill Quarry, Co. Antrim (A).
27	10.52	12.77	05.80	Crosshill Quarry, Co. Antrim (A).
28*	12.52	?	05.80	Crosshill Quarry, Co. Antrim (A).
29	12.52	12.78	05.80	Crosshill Quarry, Co. Antrim (A).
30*	03.53	?	05.80	Crosshill Quarry, Co. Antrim (A).
31	03.53	05.76	05.80	Crosshill Quarry, Co. Antrim (A).

DRIVING MOTOR BRAKE THIRD (* DRIVING MOTOR BRAKE COMPOSITE)

Built: 1953 by UTA.
Engines: Two Leyland EO 600/177 of 125 hp (93 kW) at 1800 rpm.
Transmission: Hydraulic. Two Lysholm Smith torque converters.
Seats: 61 (* 8F, 70T). **Length:** 61 ft 3 in (18.67 m).
Width: 9 ft 5 in (2.88 m). **Weight:** 34 tons.
Brakes: Air.

Used in conjunction with power cars 8–31 and trailers 501–514 & 515–528 in 3 or 4 (from 1956/7) car sets.
All were re-engined with Leyland 680 165 hp (123 kW) engines between June 1956 and January 1957 and the DMCO cars were converted at the same time to DMSO seating 85S.
The hydraulic transmissions were replaced by mechanical with Wilson 4 speed gearboxes between July and December 1968.

Vehicle No.	Month to Traffic	Month Withdrawn	Month Cut Up	Disposal Location
32	06.53	?	05.80	Crosshill Quarry, Co. Antrim (A)
33*	06.53	?	05.80	Crosshill Quarry, Co. Antrim (A)
34	07.53	?	05.80	Crosshill Quarry, Co. Antrim (A)
35*	07.53	?	05.80	Crosshill Quarry, Co. Antrim (A)

TRAILER THIRD

Built: 1952–54 by UTA.
Seats: 91.
Width: 9 ft 5 in (2.88 m).
Brakes: Air.

Length: 60 ft 4 in (18.39 m).
Weight: 26 tons.

Used in conjunction with power cars 8–35.
Originally numbered 201-214 prior to 1958.
504–509 were converted to DTSO between December 1957 and May 1958, seating 87S.
505–507 were reconverted to TSO in 1961, seating 93S, the driving equipment being subsequently fitted to 24, 26 & 28. The driving cabs were removed in 1963–64.
2 additional seats were fitted in 501–504 & 508–14 upon removal of their steam heating boilers in 1960–61, then seating 89 or 93S.
The seating layout of 510 was further modified to seat 103S, date unknown.

Vehicle No.	Month to Traffic	Month Withdrawn	Month Cut Up	Disposal Location
501	08.52	?	05.80	Crosshill Quarry, Co. Antrim (A).
502	10.52	?	05.80	Crosshill Quarry, Co. Antrim (A).
503	12.52	?	05.80	Crosshill Quarry, Co. Antrim (A).
504	02.53	?	05.80	Crosshill Quarry, Co. Antrim (A).
505	03.53	?	05.80	Crosshill Quarry, Co. Antrim (A).
506	04.53	10.73	?	?
507	06.53	?	05.80	Crosshill Quarry, Co. Antrim (A).
508	07.53	05.75	-	Converted to parcels van 631.
509	07.53	?	05.80	Crosshill Quarry, Co. Antrim (A).
510	10.53	11.77	05.80	Crosshill Quarry, Co. Antrim (A).
511	10.53	11.75	-	Converted to parcels van 634.
512	12.53	07.75	-	Converted to parcles van 632.
513	02.54	10.75	-	Converted to parcels van 633.
514	04.54	?	05.80	Crosshill Quarry, Co. Antrim (A).

506 was withdrawn following bomb damage suffered at Marino.

After being withdrawn as parcels vans, 631–634 were sent to Crosshill Quarry, 631 in October 1983 and the others in January 1985 (A).

TRAILER BRAKE THIRD

Built: 1953 by UTA.
Seats: 80.
Width: 9 ft 5 in (2.88 m).
Brakes: Air, vacuum piped.

Length: 60 ft 4 in (18.39 m).
Weight: 24 tons.

Used in conjunction with railcar 5.
Numbered 215 prior to 1958.
After railcar 5 was withdrawn, gangway ends were fitted in March 1968, seating ? S.
The seating layout was further modified in January 1972, seating 68S.

Vehicle No.	Month to Traffic	Month Withdrawn	Month Cut Up	Disposal Location
515	.54	11.77	05.80	Crosshill Quarry, Co. Antrim (A).

TRAILER STANDARD (COMPARTMENT)

Built: 1956 by UTA.
Seats: 108.
Width: 9 ft (2.74 m).
Brakes: Air.

Length: 57 ft 1 in (17.40 m).
Weight: 30 tons (* 28 tons).

Converted from J11 class loco hauled coaches 169, 173, 174, 176, 177, 181, 186, 187, 189 & 191 respectively, built 1925–38.
519 was converted to TSO seating 72S in May 1968.
523 was converted to TSO seating 64S in August 1968.
The 28 ton vehicles had wooden bodies, the others steel.

Vehicle No.	Month to Traffic	Month Withdrawn	Month Cut Up	Disposal Location
516	06.56	06.70	?	?
517*	12.56	06.73	?	?
518*	11.56	12.70	?	?
519*	05.56	.74	.80	Antrim
520	05.56	?	09.70	Belfast Queen's Quay
521	05.56	06.70	?	?
522	06.56	?	09.70	Belfast Queen's Quay
523	06.56	?	.80	Antrim
524	12.56	06.73	?	?
525*	06.56	09.70	?	?

TRAILER STANDARD

Built: 1956–57 by UTA.
Seats: 80.　　　　　　　　　　　　　**Length:** 57 ft 1 in (17.40 m).
Width: 9 ft 4 in (2.85 m).　　　　　**Weight:** 28 tons.
Brakes: Air, vacuum piped.

Converted from J5 class timber bodied loco hauled coaches 255 & 261 respectively, built 1929–30.
Converted to MPD TSO in August 1962.
526 was transferred to the RPSI reserve fleet on 04.05.79 to be refurbished. However, this project was soon abandoned but the vehicle was retained for preservation by the RPSI.

Vehicle No.	Month to Traffic	Month Withdrawn	Month Cut Up	Disposal Location
526	03.57	05.79	-	RPSI Depot, Whitehead (P).
527	10.56	11.77	02.78	Magheramorne.

TRAILER THIRD (COMPARTMENT)

Built: 1951 by UTA.
Seats: 120.　　　　　　　　　　　　**Length:**
Width: 9 ft 5 in (2.88 m).　　　　　**Weight:** 31 tons.
Brakes: Air.

Converted from J7 class loco hauled coach 279, built 1933.
Used in conjunction with power cars 6 & 7.

Vehicle No.	Month to Traffic	Month Withdrawn	Month Cut Up	Disposal Location
528	08.51	12.77	?	?

MULTI PURPOSE DIESEL MULTIPLE UNITS (MPD).
DRIVING MOTOR BRAKE STANDARD

Built: 1957–58 by UTA.
Engine: Leyland O900 of 275 hp (205 kW) at 1800 rpm.
Transmission: Hydraulic. Schneider torque converter.
Seats: 47.　　　　　　　　　　　　　**Length:** 57 ft 9 in (17.61 m).
Width: 9 ft 5 in (2.88 m).　　　　　**Weight:** 39 tons.
Brakes: Air, vacuum piped.

Converted from J17 class loco hauled coaches 321, 322, 323 & 326 respectively, built 1951.
36 & 39 were re-engined with an AEC AH1100/6 260 hp (194 kW) engine, dates unknown.
38 was re-engined with a Rolls Royce C6.TFLH Mark IV engine of 260 hp (194 kW) at 1800 rpm in September 1964.

Vehicle No.	Month to Traffic	Month Withdrawn	Month Cut Up	Disposal Location
36	09.57	04.78	10.78	Magheramorne.
37	09.57	07.68	?	?
38	12.57	12.77	?	?
39	01.58	.78	09.80	Nutts Corner Airport.

37 was withdrawn following fire damage suffered at Ballymena on 24.07.68 whilst working the 0710 Portrush to Belfast York Road service.

The bodyshell of 39 was used as a storage shed at Nutts Corner Airport until September 1980.

DRIVING MOTOR STANDARD

Built: 1957 by UTA.
Engine: Leyland O900 of 275 hp (205 kW) at 1800 rpm.
Transmission: Hydraulic. Schneider torque converter.
Seats: 54 (40), 51 (41).   **Length:** 57 ft 9 in (17.61 m).
Width: 9 ft 5 in (2.88 m).   **Weight:** 39 tons.
Brakes: Air, vacuum piped.

Converted from J17 class loco hauled coaches 324 & 325 respectively, built 1951.
Both were re-engined with an AEC AH1100/6 260 hp (194 kw) at 1800 rpm engine, dates unknown.

Vehicle No.	Month to Traffic	Month Withdrawn	Month Cut Up	Disposal Location
40	12.57	12.73	02.78	Magheramorne.
41	11.57	07.75	?	?

DRIVING MOTOR COMPOSITE (COMPARTMENT)

Built: 1957–58 by UTA.
Engine: Leyland O900 of 275 hp (205 kW) at 1800 rpm.
Transmission: Hydraulic. Schneider torque converter.
Seats: 15F, 24S.   **Length:** 57 ft 9 in (17.61 m).
Width: 9 ft 5 in (2.8 m).   **Weight:** 40 tons.
Brakes: Air, vacuum piped.

Converted from F7 class loco hauled coaches 341 & 342 respectively, built 1951.
Both were re-engined with an AEC AH1100/6 260 hp (194 kw) at 1800 rpm engine, dates unknown.

Vehicle No.	Month to Traffic	Month Withdrawn	Month Cut Up	Disposal Location
42	11.57	03.78	09.80	Nutts Corner Airport.
43	01.58	10.73	02.78	Magheramorne.

The bodyshell of 42 was used as a storage shed at Nutts Corner Airport until September 1980.

DRIVING MOTOR BRAKE STANDARD (COMPARTMENT)

Built: 1959 by UTA.
Engine: Leyland O900 of 275 hp (205 kW) at 1800 rpm.
Transmission: Hydraulic. Schneider torque converter.
Seats: 36.   **Length:** 57 ft 9 in (17.61 m).
Width: 9 ft 5 in (2.88 m).   **Weight:** 44 tons.
Brakes: Air, vacuum piped.

Converted from K6 class loco hauled coach 331, built 1951.
Re-engined with a Rolls Royce C6.TFLH Mark IV engine of 260 hp (194 kW) at 1800 rpm, date unknown.

Vehicle No.	Month to Traffic	Month Withdrawn	Month Cut Up	Disposal Location
44	10.58	08.76	?	?

DRIVING MOTOR BRAKE COMPOSITE (COMPARTMENT)

Built: 1959 by UTA.
Engine: Leyland O900 of 275 hp (205 kW) at 1800 rpm.
Transmission: Hydraulic. Schneider torque converter.
Seats: 12F, 24S.　　　　　　　　　　　**Length:** 57 ft 9 in (17.61 m).
Width: 9 ft 5 in (2.88 m).　　　　　　　**Weight:** 44 tons.
Brakes: Air, vacuum piped.

Converted from K6 class loco hauled coach 332, built 1951.
Re-engined with a Rolls Royce C6.TFLH Mark IV engine of 260 hp (194 kW) at 1800 rpm, date unknown.

Vehicle No.	Month to Traffic	Month Withdrawn	Month Cut Up	Disposal Location
45	11.59	03.78	10.78	Magheramorne.

DRIVING MOTOR BRAKE COMPOSITE (COMPARTMENT)

Built: 1958–59 by UTA.
Engine: Leyland O900 of 275 hp (205 kW) at 1800 rpm.
Transmission: Hydraulic. Schneider torque converter.
Seats: 16F, 60S.　　　　　　　　　　　**Length:** 57 ft 9 in (17.61 m).
Width: 9 ft 5 in (2.88 m).　　　　　　　**Weight:** 40 tons.
Brakes: Air, vacuum piped.

Converted from H2 class loco hauled coaches 280, 281 & 282, built 1933.
46 was re-engined with a Rolls Royce C6.TFLH Mark IV engine of 260 hp (194 kW) at 1800 rpm, date unknown.
47 & 48 were re-engined with an AEC AH1100/6 260 hp (194 kw) at 1800 rpm engine, dates unknown.
46 & 47 were converted to DMBsoC seating 16F, 44S in July 1969 and March 1970 respectively.

Vehicle No.	Month to Traffic	Month Withdrawn	Month Cut Up	Disposal Location
46	12.58	?	?	?
47	02.59	.77	?	?
48	02.59	06.76	?	?

DRIVING MOTOR BRAKE STANDARD (COMPARTMENT)

Built: 1959 by UTA.
Engine: Leyland O900 of 275 hp (205 kW) at 1800 rpm.
Transmission: Hydraulic. Schneider torque converter.
Seats: 84.　　　　　　　　　　　　　　**Length:** 57 ft 9 in (17.61 m).
Width: 9 ft 5 in (2.88 m).　　　　　　　**Weight:** 40 tons.
Brakes: Air, vacuum piped.

Converted from K7 class loco hauled coach 351, built 1951.
Re-engined with an AEC AH1100/6 260 hp (194 kw) at 1800 rpm engine, date unknown.
Converted to DMBSO seating 68S in December 1970.

Vehicle No.	Month to Traffic	Month Withdrawn	Month Cut Up	Disposal Location
49	01.59	05.79	-	Converted to hauled stock.

Converted to form part of a loco hauled excursion set for use with 101 class locomotives.

DRIVING MOTOR BRAKE STANDARD (COMPARTMENT)

Built: 1959 by UTA.
Engine: Leyland O900 of 275 hp (205 kW) at 1800 rpm.
Transmission: Hydraulic. Schneider torque converter.
Seats: 96. **Length:** 60 ft 9 in (18.53 m).
Width: 9 ft 5 in (2.88 m). **Weight:** 43 tons.
Brakes: Air, vacuum piped.

Converted from J7 class loco hauled coaches 274, 275, 276 & 277 respectively, built 1933.
Re-engined with Rolls Royce C6.TFLH Mark IV engines of 260 hp (194 kW) at 1800 rpm, dates unknown.
All were converted to DMBSO seating 78S between November 1968 and October 1969.

Vehicle No.	Month to Traffic	Month Withdrawn	Month Cut Up	Disposal Location
50	03.59	09.77	02.78	Magheramorne.
51	03.59	.80	?	?
52	03.59	.80	?	?
53	04.59	07.74	?	?

DRIVING MOTOR BRAKE COMPOSITE

Built: 1959 by UTA.
Engine: Leyland O900 of 275 hp (205 kW) at 1800 rpm.
Transmission: Hydraulic. Schneider torque converter.
Seats: 12F, 55S (54), 10F, 50S (55). **Length:** 57 ft 9 in (17.61 m).
Width: 9 ft 5 in (2.88 m). **Weight:** 40 tons.
Brakes: Air, vacuum piped.

Converted from I3 class loco hauled coaches 54 & 55 respectively, built 1931.
54 was re-engined with a Rolls Royce C6.TFLH Mark IV engine of 260 hp (194 kW) at 1800 rpm, date unknown.
55 was re-engined with an AEC AH1100/6 260 hp (194 kw) at 1800 rpm engine, date unknown.

Vehicle No.	Month to Traffic	Month Withdrawn	Month Cut Up	Disposal Location
54	04.59	10.77	?	?
55	05.59	12.77	07.78	Magheramorne.

DRIVING MOTOR BRAKE COMPOSITE

Built: 1959 by UTA.
Engine: Leyland O900 of 275 hp (205 kW) at 1800 rpm.
Transmission: Hydraulic. Schneider torque converter.
Seats: 12F, 60S. **Length:** 60 ft 9 in (18.53 m).
Width: 9 ft 5 in (2.88 m). **Weight:**
Brakes: Air, vacuum piped.

Converted from A5 class loco hauled coach 3, built 1944.
Re-engined with an AEC AH1100/6 260 hp (194 kw) at 1800 rpm engine in April 1964.

Vehicle No.	Month to Traffic	Month Withdrawn	Month Cut Up	Disposal Location
56	08.59	07.66	?	?

Withdrawn following fire damage suffered at Brookmount.

DRIVING MOTOR BRAKE STANDARD

Built: 1959 by UTA.
Engine: Leyland O900 of 275 hp (205 kW) at 1800 rpm.
Transmission: Hydraulic. Schneider torque converter.
Seats: 70. **Length:** 57 ft 9 in (17.61 m).
Width: 9 ft 5 in (2.88 m). **Weight:** 40 tons.
Brakes: Air, vacuum piped.

Converted from J6 class loco hauled coaches 265–270 respectively, built 1932–35.
All except 58 were re-engined with a Rolls Royce C6.TFLH Mark IV engine of 260 hp (194 kW) at 1800 rpm, dates unknown.

Vehicle No.	Month to Traffic	Month Withdrawn	Month Cut Up	Disposal Location
57	05.59	05.77	02.78	Magheramorne
58	06.59	07.59	?	?
59	06.59	.80	?	?
60	07.59	02.78	10.78	Magheramorne
61	07.59	05.79	-	Converted to hauled stock.
62	07.59	07.77	09.80	Nutts Corner Airport.

58 was withdrawn following a collision with a motor car at Downhill accommodation crossing on 18.07.59.
61 was converted to form part of a loco hauled excursion set for use with 101 class locomotives.
The bodyshell of 62 was used as a storage shed at Nutts Corner Airport until September 1980.

DRIVING MOTOR BRAKE STANDARD

Built: 1961–62 by UTA.
Engine: Leyland O900 of 275 hp (205 kW) at 1800 rpm.
Transmission: Hydraulic. Schneider torque converter.
Seats: 70. **Length:** 61 ft 6 in (18.75 m).
Width: 9 ft 5 in (2.88 m). **Weight:** 43 tons.
Brakes: Air, vacuum piped.

Converted from I4 class loco hauled coaches 252, 254 & 256 respectively, built 1938.
Re-engined with Rolls Royce C6.TFLH Mark IV engines of 260 hp (194 kW) at 1800 rpm, dates unknown.

Vehicle No.	Month to Traffic	Month Withdrawn	Month Cut Up	Disposal Location
63	11.61	?	10.83	Crosshill Quarry, Co. Antrim (A).
64	12.61	.84	08.85	Crosshill Quarry, Co. Antrim (A).
65	02.62	.79	10.83	Crosshill Quarry, Co. Antrim (A).

DRIVING TRAILER STANDARD (COMPARTMENT)

Built: 1959 by UTA.
Seats: 42. **Length:** 57 ft 9 in (17.61 m).
Width: 9 ft 5 in (2.88 m). **Weight:** 30 tons.
Brakes: Air, vacuum piped.

Converted from J16 class loco hauled coaches 303, 301, 302, 304–306 respectivley, built 1951.

Vehicle No.	Month to Traffic	Month Withdrawn	Month Cut Up	Disposal Location
529	02.59	.77	07.78	Magheramorne.
530	04.59	.78	?	?
531	06.59	.77	?	?
532	04.59	04.78	?	?
533	04.59	04.78	-	Body to 583.
534	05.59	10.76	-	Converted to 728 (qv).

After withdrawal the bodyshell of 533 was fitted to the underframe of 583, whose body had been destroyed by fire. The underframe of 533 was converted to a conflat wagon.

▲ MPD car no. 41 leads a seven car set away from Ballymoney with a Sunday School excursion returning from Portrush to Belfast in May 1975.

Jonathan Allen

▼ 70 Class power car no. 71 pulls away from Larne Town station with the 1255 to Belfast York Road on 29th May 1977. The centre car is unidentified, but the driving trailer is no. 714.

Jonathan Allen

DRIVING TRAILER STANDARD (COMPARTMENT)

Built: 1959 by UTA.
Seats: 96.
Width: 8 ft 11 in (2.72 m).
Brakes: Air, vacuum piped.

Length: 57 ft 9 in (17.61 m).
Weight: 30 tons.

Converted from J11 class loco hauled coaches 188 & 195 respectively, built 1937 and 1939 respectively.
Rebuilt to TSO seating 64S in March and June 1971 respectively, length then reduced to 57 ft 1 in (17.40 m).

Vehicle No.	Month to Traffic	Month Withdrawn	Month Cut Up	Disposal Location
535	06.59	05.79	-	Converted to hauled stock.
536	07.59	05.79	-	Converted to hauled stock.

Converted to form part of a loco hauled excursion set for use with 101 class locomotives.

DRIVING TRAILER STANDARD (COMPARTMENT)

Built: 1959 by UTA.
Seats: 102.
Width: 9 ft 5 in (2.88 m).
Brakes: Air, vacuum piped.

Length: 57 ft 9 in (17.61 m).
Weight: 31 tons.

Converted from K2 class loco hauled coaches 271–273 respectively, built 1933.
Rebuilt to TSO seating 68S in April 1970, March 1969 & August 1971 respectively.

Vehicle No.	Month to Traffic	Month Withdrawn	Month Cut Up	Disposal Location
537	07.59	?	02.78	Magheramorne.
538	08.59	?	?	?
539	09.59	05.79	-	Converted to hauled stock.

539 was converted to form part of a loco hauled excursion set for use with 101 class locomotives.

DRIVING TRAILER STANDARD

Built: 1959 by UTA.
Seats: 85.
Width: 9 ft 5 in (2.88 m).
Brakes: Air, vacuum piped.

Length: 57 ft 9 in (17.61 m).
Weight: 29 tons.

Converted from J6 class loco hauled coaches 229 & 231 respectively, built 1935.

Vehicle No.	Month to Traffic	Month Withdrawn	Month Cut Up	Disposal Location
540	10.59	05.79	-	Converted to hauled stock.
541	10.59	05.79	-	Converted to hauled stock.

Converted to form part of a loco hauled excursion set for use with 101 class locomotives.

DRIVING TRAILER COMPOSITE

Built: 1959 by UTA.
Seats: 12F, 65S.
Width: 9 ft 5 in (2.88 m).
Brakes: Air, vacuum piped.

Length: 57 ft 9 in (17.61 m).
Weight: 29 tons.

Converted from I3 class loco hauled coach 57, built 1931.

Vehicle No.	Month to Traffic	Month Withdrawn	Month Cut Up	Disposal Location
542	10.59	05.79	-	Converted to hauled stock.

Converted to form part of a loco hauled excursion set for use with 101 class locomotives.

DRIVING TRAILER COMPOSITE (COMPARTMENT)

Built: 1959 by UTA.
Seats: 32F, 36S.
Width: 9 ft 5 in (2.88 m).
Brakes: Air, vacuum piped.

Length: 57 ft 9 in (17.61 m).
Weight: 31 tons.

Converted from F8 class loco hauled coach 361, built 1951.

Vehicle No.	Month to Traffic	Month Withdrawn	Month Cut Up	Disposal Location
543	05.59	.74	10.74	Belfast York Road.

The cutting up date above relates to the body only. The underframe was converted to a Conflat wagon.

TRAILER THIRD

Built:
Seats: 100.
Width: 9 ft 5¼ in (2.88 m).
Brakes: Vacuum.

Length: 62 ft (18.90 m).
Weight: 17.5 tons.

Converted from NCC trailer thirds 1 & 2 respectively, built 1934 (qv).

Vehicle No.	Month to Traffic	Month Withdrawn	Month Cut Up	Disposal Location
544	?	?	?	?
545	?	?	-	Converted to signals van 3109.

TRAILER BUFFET FIRST

Built: 1960 by UTA.
Seats: 32F.
Width: 9 ft 6 in (2.90 m).
Brakes: Air, vacuum piped.

Length: 57 ft (17.37 m).
Weight: 31.5 tons.

Converted from B2 class loco hauled coach 88, built 1924.
Declassified to standard class April 1964.
Modified for operation with 70 Class vehicles in 1966.

Vehicle No.	Month to Traffic	Month Withdrawn	Month Cut Up	Disposal Location
548	05.60	10.72	?	?

TRAILER BUFFET FIRST

Built: 1957 by UTA.
Seats: 32F.
Width: 9 ft 6 in (2.90 m).
Brakes: Air, vacuum piped.

Length: 60 ft 1 in (18.31 m).
Weight: 30 tons.

Converted from B4 class loco hauled coach 90, built 1934.
Declassified to standard class April 1964.

Vehicle No.	Month to Traffic	Month Withdrawn	Month Cut Up	Disposal Location
549	05.57	06.70	?	?

TRAILER BUFFET FIRST

Built: 1957 by UTA.
Seats: 30F.
Width: 9 ft 5¼ in (2.88 m).
Brakes: Air, vacuum piped.

Length: 60 ft 1 in (18.31 m).
Weight: 31 tons.

Converted from B5 class loco hauled coach 87, built 1950.
Declassified to standard class seating 34S in April 1964.
Modified for operation with 70 Class vehicles, date unknown.

Vehicle No.	Month to Traffic	Month Withdrawn	Month Cut Up	Disposal Location
550	.57	.78	-	RPSI Depot, Whitehead (P).

550 has been reconverted to loco hauled coach 87 by the RPSI and is used in their "Enterprise" rake of coaches.

TRAILER BUFFET STANDARD

Built: 1958 by UTA.
Seats: 27S.   **Length:** 58 ft 0¾ in (17.70 m).
Width: 9 ft 6 in (2.90 m).   **Weight:** 32 tons.
Brakes: Vacuum.

Converted from B8 class loco hauled coach 266, built 1936.

Vehicle No.	Month to Traffic	Month Withdrawn	Month Cut Up	Disposal Location
551	05.58	?	?	?

TRAILER BUFFET COMPOSITE

Built: 1957 by UTA.
Seats: 12F, 18S.   **Length:** 58 ft 0¾ in (17.70 m).
Width: 9 ft 6 in (2.90 m).   **Weight:** 32.5 tons.
Brakes: Vacuum.

Converted from B6 class loco hauled coach 88, built 1938.
Converted to TBSO seating 30S in March 1962.

Vehicle No.	Month to Traffic	Month Withdrawn	Month Cut Up	Disposal Location
552	12.57	?	?	?

TRAILER BUFFET STANDARD

Built: 1957 by UTA.
Seats: 24.   **Length:** 58 ft 0¾ in (17.70 m).
Width: 9 ft 6 in (2.90 m).   **Weight:** 30 tons.
Brakes: Vacuum.

Converted from B9 class loco hauled coach 124, built 1942.

Vehicle No.	Month to Traffic	Month Withdrawn	Month Cut Up	Disposal Location
553	06.57	04.71	?	?

TRAILER BUFFET STANDARD

Built: 1957 by UTA.
Seats: 24.   **Length:** 60 ft 0¾ in (18.31 m).
Width: 9 ft 6 in (2.90 m).   **Weight:** 31 tons.
Brakes: Vacuum.

Converted from B4 class loco hauled coach 403, built 1950.
Modified for operation with 70 class vehicles July 1969.

Vehicle No.	Month to Traffic	Month Withdrawn	Month Cut Up	Disposal Location
554	11.57	.70	?	?

TRAILER BUFFET STANDARD

Built: 1950 by UTA.
Seats: 44.
Width: 9 ft 6 in (2.90 m).
Brakes: Vacuum.

Length: 58 ft 0¾ in (17.70 m).
Weight: 29.5 tons.

Converted from K23 class loco hauled coach 188, built 1943.
Re-seated to 72 seats in June 1967.

Vehicle No.	Month to Traffic	Month Withdrawn	Month Cut Up	Disposal Location
555	06.50	.72	?	?

TRAILER BUFFET STANDARD

Built: 1958 by UTA.
Seats: 72.
Width: 9 ft 6 in (2.90 m).
Brakes: Vacuum.

Length: 58 ft 0¾ in (17.70 m).
Weight: 29.5 tons.

Converted from K23 class loco hauled coach 127, built 1951.

Vehicle No.	Month to Traffic	Month Withdrawn	Month Cut Up	Disposal Location
556	10.58	05.69	-	Converted to 70 Class TSK 727 (qv)

TRAILER FIRST (COMPARTMENT)

Built: 1957 by UTA.
Seats: 36.
Width: 9 ft 6 in (2.90 m).
Brakes: Vacuum.

Length: 60 ft 0¾ in (18.31 m).
Weight: 32.5 tons.

Converted from C2 class loco hauled coach 227, built 1949.
Converted to TCK seating 18F, 24S in March 1961.

Vehicle No.	Month to Traffic	Month Withdrawn	Month Cut Up	Disposal Location
561	09.57	?	-	RPSI Depot, Whitehead (P).

TRAILER BRAKE FIRST (COMPARTMENT)

Built: 1957 by UTA.
Seats: 18.
Width: 9 ft 6 in (2.90 m).
Brakes: Vacuum.

Length: 60 ft 0¾ in (18.31 m).
Weight: 34.75 tons.

Converted from D5 class loco hauled coach 231, built 1948.

Vehicle No.	Month to Traffic	Month Withdrawn	Month Cut Up	Disposal Location
562	12.57	?	?	?

TRAILER COMPOSITE (COMPARTMENT)

Built: 1957–58 by UTA.
Seats: 24F, 24S.
Width: 9 ft 6 in (2.90 m).
Brakes: Vacuum.

Length: 58 ft 0¾ in (17.70 m).
Weight: 31.5 tons.

Converted from F16 class loco hauled coaches 20, 29 & 89 respectively, built 1935–39.
571 was converted to TSK seating 56S date unknown.
572 was converted to TBFK seating 18F date unknown.

Vehicle No.	Month to Traffic	Month Withdrawn	Month Cut Up	Disposal Location
571	12.57	?	?	?
572	09.58	?	?	?
573	01.58	?	05.75	Antrim.

TRAILER STANDARD

Built: 1962 by UTA.
Seats: 70.
Width: 9 ft 6 in (2.90 m).
Brakes: Vacuum.

Length: 58 ft 0¾ in (17.70 m).
Weight: 29 tons.

Converted from loco hauled coach 145, built 1948.

Vehicle No.	Month to Traffic	Month Withdrawn	Month Cut Up	Disposal Location
580	02.62	.72	?	?

TRAILER STANDARD

Built: 1951 (581) or 1957–58 (582–4) by UTA.
Seats: 70.
Width: 9 ft 6 in (2.90 m).
Brakes: Vacuum.

Length: 58 ft 0¾ in (17.70 m).
Weight: 29 tons.

Converted from K15 class loco hauled coaches 98 (built 1941), 186 (built 1946), 176 & 177 (both built 1947) respectively.

Vehicle No.	Month to Traffic	Month Withdrawn	Month Cut Up	Disposal Location
581	01.51	.72	-	RPSI Depot, Whitehead (P).
582	10.58	.72	?	?
583	06.57	?	-	RPSI Depot, Whitehead (P).
584	07.57	?	05.75	Antrim

The original body of 583 was destroyed by fire on 23.03.78 and the body ex 533 was subsequently fitted to the underframe.

TRAILER STANDARD

Built: 1954 by UTA.
Seats: 72.
Width: 9 ft 6 in (2.90 m).
Brakes: Vacuum.

Length: 60 ft 0¾ in (18.31 m).
Weight: 29.5 tons.

Converted from K31 class loco hauled coaches 8 & 9 respectively, built 1954.

Vehicle No.	Month to Traffic	Month Withdrawn	Month Cut Up	Disposal Location
585	03.54	04.71	?	?
586	04.54	?	-	RPSI Depot, Whitehead (P).

586 has been reconverted to loco hauled coach 9 by the RPSI and is used in their "Enterprise" rake of coaches.

TRAILER BRAKE STANDARD

Built: 1958 by UTA.
Seats: 21.
Width: 9 ft 6 in (2.90 m).
Brakes: Vacuum.

Length: 58 ft 0¾ in (17.70 m).
Weight: 31.5 tons.

Converted from L12 class loco hauled coaches 53 (built 1937) & 94 (built 1939) respectively.

Vehicle No.	Month to Traffic	Month Withdrawn	Month Cut Up	Disposal Location
591	04.58	?	?	?
592	01.58	?	?	?

TRAILER BRAKE STANDARD

Built: 1950 by UTA.
Seats: 39.
Width: 9 ft 6 in (2.90 m).
Brakes: Vacuum.

Length: 58 ft 0¾ in (17.70 m).
Weight: 31.25 tons.

Converted from L13 class loco hauled coach 115, built 1940.

Vehicle No.	Month to Traffic	Month Withdrawn	Month Cut Up	Disposal Location
593	11.50	.72	?	?

TRAILER BRAKE STANDARD

Built: 1958 by UTA.
Seats: 21.
Width: 9 ft 6 in (2.90 m).
Brakes: Vacuum.

Length: 58 ft 0¾ in (17.70 m).
Weight: 28 tons.

Converted from L4 class loco hauled coaches 175 & 189 respectively, built 1946.

Vehicle No.	Month to Traffic	Month Withdrawn	Month Cut Up	Disposal Location
594	06.58	?	?	?
595	07.58	?	-	RPSI Depot, Whitehead (P).

UTA/NIR DIESEL ELECTRIC MULTIPLE UNITS
70 CLASS
DRIVING MOTOR STANDARD

Built: 1966–68 by UTA.
Engine: English Electric 4SRKT turbocharged of 550 hp (410 kW) at 850 rpm.
Traction Motors: Two EE 538 of 220 hp (164 kW) mounted on power car bogie remote from the engine.
Seats: 44.
Width: 9 ft 5 in (2.88 m).
Brakes: Air, vacuum piped.

Length: 64 ft 6 in (19.66 m).
Weight: 61.8 tons.

From 1976 onwards all vehicles were re-seated to seat 53.
The power equipment from these cars is now fitted to the Castle Class power cars.

Vehicle No.	Month to Traffic	Month Withdrawn	Month Cut Up	Disposal Location
71	07.66	01.85	08.85	Crosshill Quarry, Co. Antrim (A).
72	07.66	09.85	08.86	Crosshill Quarry, Co. Antrim (A).
73	10.66	05.85	08.85	Crosshill Quarry, Co. Antrim (A).
74	10.66	04.84	01.85	Crosshill Quarry, Co. Antrim (A).
75	11.66	04.86	08.86	Crosshill Quarry, Co. Antrim (A).
76	02.67	09.84	01.85	Crosshill Quarry, Co. Antrim (A).

| 77 | 04.67 | 04.86 | 08.86 | Crosshill Quarry, Co. Antrim (A). |
| 78 | 09.68 | 05.79 | 05.80 | Crosshill Quarry, Co. Antrim (A). |

Names

71	RIVER BUSH	75	RIVER MAINE
72	RIVER FOYLE	76	RIVER INVER
73	RIVER ROE	77	RIVER BRAID
74	RIVER LAGAN	78	RIVER BANN

72 was painted in Sealink livery for a time immediately prior to withdrawal.

75 & 77 were withdrawn after suffering vandal damage on 01.04.86.

78 was withdrawn after suffering fire bomb damage at Belfast York Road on 25.05.79.

TRAILER BRAKE FIRST (COMPARTMENT)

Built: 1966 by UTA.
Seats: 24.
Width: 9 ft 5 in (2.88 m).
Brakes: Air, vacuum piped.
Length: 57 ft 4 in (17.48 m).
Weight: 30 tons.

Converted to DBSO seating 58S in December 1977.
The frame for this vehicle was constructed in 1930.

Vehicle No.	Month to Traffic	Month Withdrawn	Month Cut Up	Disposal Location
701	06.66	04.86	08.86	Crosshill Quarry, Co. Antrim (A).

This vehicle was painted in Sealink livery for a time immediately prior to withdrawal, which was occasioned following vandal damage on 01.04.86.

TRAILER BRAKE COMPOSITE (COMPARTMENT)

Built: 1966 by UTA.
Seats: 12F, 16S.
Width: 9 ft 5 in (2.88 m).
Brakes: Air, vacuum piped.
Length: 57 ft 4 in (17.48 m).
Weight: 30 tons.

The frame for this vehicle was constructed in 1929.

Vehicle No.	Month to Traffic	Month Withdrawn	Month Cut Up	Disposal Location
702	09.66	.84	01.85	Crosshill Quarry, Co. Antrim (A).

TRAILER BRAKE STANDARD (COMPARTMENT)

Built: 1966 by UTA.
Seats: 32.
Width: 9 ft 5 in (2.88 m).
Brakes: Air, vacuum piped.
Length: 57 ft 4 in (17.48 m).
Weight: 30 tons.

Converted to DTBSO seating 58S in November 1977.
The frame for this vehicle was constructed in 1928.

Vehicle No.	Month to Traffic	Month Withdrawn	Month Cut Up	Disposal Location
703	03.67	?	01.85	Crosshill Quarry, Co. Antrim (A).

DRIVING TRAILER BRAKE COMPOSITE (COMPARTMENT)

Built: 1966 by UTA.
Seats: 12F, 24S.
Width: 9 ft 5 in (2.88 m).
Brakes: Air, vacuum piped.
Length: 57 ft 4 in (17.48 m).
Weight: 30 tons.

The frames for these vehicles were constructed in 1928.
Both vehicles were converted to DTBSO seating 63S in 1976.

Vehicle No.	Month to Traffic	Month Withdrawn	Month Cut Up	Disposal Location
711	05.66	?	08.85	Crosshill Quarry, Co. Antrim (A).
712	10.66	03.83	10.83	Crosshill Quarry, Co. Antrim (A).

712 was withdrawn after an accident at Hilden on 25.03.83.

DRIVING TRAILER BRAKE STANDARD (COMPARTMENT)

Built: 1968 by UTA.
Seats: 40.
Width: 9 ft (2.74 m).
Brakes: Air, vacuum piped.
Length: 57 ft 1 in (17.40 m).
Weight: 29 tons.

Converted from F2 class loco hauled coaches 278 & 280, built 1924.
713 was converted to DTBSO seating 63S in July 1977.
714 was converted to DTBSO seating 49S in May 1978.

Vehicle No.	Month to Traffic	Month Withdrawn	Month Cut Up	Disposal Location
713	11.68	.84	-	Belfast York Road.
714	10.69	07.79	07.80	Magheramorne.

714 was withdrawn after an accident at Dunloy on 09.07.79.

TRAILER STANDARD (COMPARTMENT)

Built: 1966 by UTA.
Seats: 56.
Width: 9 ft 5 in (2.88 m).
Brakes: Air, vacuum piped.
Length: 57 ft 4 in (17.48 m).
Weight: 30 tons.

The frames for these vehicles were constructed 1925–32.

Vehicle No.	Month to Traffic	Month Withdrawn	Month Cut Up	Disposal Location
721	03.66	04.86	08.86	Crosshill Quarry, Co. Antrim (A).
722	03.66	05.79	05.80	Crosshill Quarry, Co. Antrim (A).
723	03.66	?	08.85	Crosshill Quarry, Co. Antrim (A).
724	05.66	04.86	08.86	Crosshill Quarry, Co. Antrim (A).
725	03.66	04.86	08.86	Crosshill Quarry, Co. Antrim (A).

721, 724 & 725 were withdrawn after suffering vandal damage on 01.04.86.

722 was withdrawn after suffering fire bomb damage at Belfast York Road on 25.05.79.

725 was painted in Sealink livery for a time immediately prior to withdrawal.

TRAILER STANDARD (COMPARTMENT)

Built: 1969 by NIR.
Seats: 64.
Width: 9 ft 6 in (2.90 m).
Brakes: Air, vacuum piped.
Length: 57 ft (17.37 m).
Weight: 29 tons.

Converted from J6 class loco hauled coach 362, built 1932.
Converted to TSO seating 70S in July 1976.

Vehicle No.	Month to Traffic	Month Withdrawn	Month Cut Up	Disposal Location
726	03.69	03.83	?	?

This vehicle was withdrawn after an accident at Hilden on 25.03.83.

▲ GNR(I) AEC power car no. 113 awaits its fate at CIE's Mullingar scrapyard during May 1975.
Jonathan Allen

▼ Unique single unit railcar no. 2509 awaits restoration at Mallow in September 1989.
Andrew Marshall

TRAILER STANDARD (COMPARTMENT)

Built: 1969 by NIR.
Seats: 72.
Width: 9 ft (2.74 m).
Brakes: Air, vacuum piped.

Length: 58 ft (17.68 m).
Weight: 29.5 tons.

Converted from trailer buffet standard 556, built 1951.

Vehicle No.	Month to Traffic	Month Withdrawn	Month Cut Up	Disposal Location
727	05.69	.80	-	RPSI Depot, Whitehead (P).

TRAILER STANDARD

Built: 1976 by NIR.
Seats: 70.
Width: 9 ft 5 in (2.88 m).
Brakes: Air, vacuum piped.

Length: 57 ft (17.37 m).
Weight: 29 tons.

Converted from driving trailer 534 (qv).
Converted to TBSO date unknown.

Vehicle No.	Month to Traffic	Month Withdrawn	Month Cut Up	Disposal Location
728	10.76	04.86	-	Belfast York Road.

This vehicle was withdrawn after suffering vandal damage on 01.04.86.

GNR (I) MULTIPLE UNITS

DRIVING MOTOR BRAKE COMPOSITE

Built: 1950–2 by GNR (I) at Dundalk Works, to a design by Park Royal Vehicles, London.
Engine: Two AEC A215 of 125 hp (93 kW) at 1800 rpm.
Transmission: Mechanical. SCG 5 speed gearbox.
Seats: 12F, 32S.
Width: 9 ft 6 in (2.90 m).
Brakes: Vacuum.

Length: 62 ft 6 in (19.05 m).
Weight: 38.25 tons (* 39.5 tons).

* fitted with Spanner train heating boiler.

GNR (I) Vehicle No.	UTA/CIE§ Vehicle No.	Month to Traffic	Month Withdrawn	Month Cut Up	Disposal Location
600*	600N§	06.50	?	?	Mullingar Scrapyard
601	601N§	06.50	?	?	Mullingar Scrapyard
602*	112	07.50	?	05.75	Antrim
603	111	07.50	?	?	?
604*	604N§	08.50	?	?	Mullingar Scrapyard
605	605N§	08.50	?	?	Mullingar Scrapyard
606*	114	09.50	.74	-	Converted to parcels van 621.
607	113	09.50	09.73		Mullingar Scrapyard
608*	608N§	10.50	?	?	Mullingar Scrapyard
609	609N§	10.50	?	?	Mullingar Scrapyard
610*	116	11.50	09.73	?	?
611	115	11.50	?	05.75	Antrim
612*	612N§	12.50	?	?	Mullingar Scrapyard
613	613N§	12.50	?	?	Mullingar Scrapyard
614*	118	12.50	?	05.75	Antrim
615	117	12.50	?	05.75	Antrim
616*	616N§	01.51	?	?	Mullingar Scrapyard
617	617N§	01.51	?	?	Mullingar Scrapyard
618*	120	04.51	.74	-	Converted to parcels van 622.
619	119	04.51	?	?	?

After withdrawal as parcels vans, 621 & 622 were cut up at Ballymena, date unknown.

DRIVING MOTOR STANDARD

Built: 1957–8 by GNR (I) at Dundalk Works, to a design by Park Royal Vehicles, London.
Engine: Two BUT A230 of 150 hp (112 kW) at 1800 rpm.
Transmission: Mechanical. SCG 4 speed gearbox.
Seats: 56.   **Length:** 65 ft 6 in (19.96 m).
Width: 9 ft 5 in (2.88 m).   **Weight:** 41 tons.
Brakes: Vacuum.

GNR (I) Vehicle No.	UTA/CIE§ Vehicle No.	Month to Traffic	Month Withdrawn	Month Cut Up	Disposal Location
701	121	06.57	?	05.80	Crosshill Quarry, Co. Antrim (A).
702	122	06.57	?	05.80	Crosshill Quarry, Co. Antrim (A).
703	123	06.57	?	05.80	Crosshill Quarry, Co. Antrim (A).
704	704N§	06.57	?	?	Mullingar Scrapyard
705	124	07.57	?	05.80	Crosshill Quarry, Co. Antrim (A).
706	706N§	07.57	?	?	Mullingar Scrapyard
707	125	09.57	?	05.80	Crosshill Quarry, Co. Antrim (A).
708	708N§	09.57	?	?	Mullingar Scrapyard
709	126	10.57	?	05.80	Crosshill Quarry, Co. Antrim (A).
710	710N§	10.57	?	?	Mullingar Scrapyard
711	127	01.58	?	05.80	Crosshill Quarry, Co. Antrim (A).
712	712N§	01.58	?	?	Mullingar Scrapyard
713	128	03.58	?	05.80	Crosshill Quarry, Co. Antrim (A).
714	714N§	03.58	?	?	Mullingar Scrapyard
715	129	05.58	?	05.80	Crosshill Quarry, Co. Antrim (A).
716	716N§	05.58	?	?	Mullingar Scrapyard

DRIVING MOTOR COMPOSITE

Built: 1958 by GNR (I) at Dundalk Works, to a design by Park Royal Vehicles, London.
Engine: Two BUT A230 of 150 hp (112 kW) at 1800 rpm.
Transmission: Mechanical. SCG 4 speed gearbox.
Seats: 16F, 40S (* 12F, 40S).   **Length:** 65 ft (19.81 m).
Width: 9 ft 5 in (2.88 m).   **Weight:** 38.25 tons.
Brakes: Vacuum.

GNR (I) Vehicle No.	UTA/CIE§ Vehicle No.	Month to Traffic	Month Withdrawn	Month Cut Up	Disposal Location
901	131	07.58	?	05.75	Antrim
902*	132	07.58	?	03.75	Antrim
903*	133	08.58	03.72	?	?
904	904N§	08.58	?	?	Mullingar Scrapyard
905	134	09.58	?	03.75	Antrim
906	906N§	09.58	?	?	Mullingar Scrapyard
907*	135	10.58	?	03.75	Antrim
908	908N§	10.58	?	?	Mullingar Scrapyard

133 was withdrawn following bomb damage suffered at Great Victoria Street on 27.03.72.

Part of 134 is now in use as a garden shed and is visible on the down side of the line near Monkstown.

CIE RAILCAR & MULTIPLE UNIT STOCK
DRIVING MOTOR BRAKE THIRD

Built: 1947 by Walker Brothers, Wigan for the Sligo, Leitrim & Northern Counties Railway.
Engines: Gardner Duo-directional of 117 hp (87 kW).
Transmission: Mechanical. Wilson epicyclic gearbox.
Seats: 59.   **Length:** 47 ft 1½ in (14.36 m).
Width: 9 ft 6 in (2.90 m).   **Weight:** 18.6 tons.
Brakes:

Formerly SL & NCR railcar "B", being purchased by CIE in October 1958. This vehicle was articulated, with a four wheel bogie underneath the driving cab which also contained the power unit, and another four wheel bogie under the passenger section.
Fitted with manually operated sliding doors.

Vehicle No.	Date to Traffic	Date Withdrawn	Month Reinstated	Date Withdrawn	Disposal Location
2509	09.07.47	01.10.57	07.59	18.09.71	GSRPS, Mallow (P).

This vehicle was latterly used as an Inspection Saloon and route learning vehicle based at Limerick Junction, and was stored there for a number of years prior to purchase by the GSRPS in 1986.

DRIVING MOTOR BRAKE COMPOSITE

Built: 1951–54 by AEC/Park Royal Vehicles, London.
Engines: Two AEC of 250 hp (186 kW).
Transmission: Mechanical. SCG 5 speed gearbox.
Seats: 12F, 32T (Mainline style).   **Length:** 62 ft 6 in (19.05 m).
Width: 9 ft 6 in (2.90 m).   **Weight:** 38.5 tons.
Brakes: Vacuum.

† Fitted with Spanner Swirlyflow 500 lbs/hr boiler.
* Converted to suburban DMBSO seating 70S in 1971.
§ Converted to suburban DMSO seating 91S in 1971.
+ Converted to suburban DMSO seating 83S in 1971.
£ Converted to suburban DMBSO seating 78S in 1971.
$ Converted to suburban DMSO seating 85S in 1971.

Vehicle No.	Month to Traffic	Month Withdrawn	Month Cut Up	Disposal Location
2600†*	.52	.73	-	Converted to push/pull DSO 6109
2601§	.52	.75	?	Mullingar Scrapyard
2602†*	.52	.72	-	Converted to push/pull CSO 6203
2603§	.52	.75	?	Mullingar Scrapyard
2604†	.52	.73	-	Converted to push/pull DSO 6108
2605+	.52	.72	-	Converted to push/pull SO 6302
2606†*	.52	.71	-	Converted to push/pull CSO 6201
2607	.52	.72	-	Converted to push/pull SO 6309
2608†	.52	.72	-	Converted to push/pull DSO 6104
2609§	.52	.73	-	Converted to push/pull SO 6327
2610†	.52	.72	-	Converted to push/pull CSO 6204
2611*	.52	.73	-	Converted to push/pull SO 6325
2612†	.52	08.57	?	Mullingar Scrapyard.
2613*	.52	.73	-	Converted to push/pull SO 6323
2614†	.52	.61	-	Converted MS 2666 (qv)
2615+	.52	.72	-	Converted to push/pull SO 6318
2616†*	.52	.73	-	Converted to push/pull CSO 6212
2617	.52	.61	-	Converted MS 2667 (qv)
2618†	.52	.72	-	Converted to push/pull DSO 6103
2619	.53	.72	-	Converted to push/pull SO 6306
2620†	.53	.73	-	Converted to push/pull DSO 6112
2621+	.53	.72	-	Converted to push/pull SO 6304
2622†£	.53	.73	-	Converted to push/pull DSO 6110

Vehicle No.	Month to Traffic	Month Withdrawn	Month Cut Up	Disposal Location
2623§	.53	.73	-	Converted to push/pull SO 6331
2624†£	.53	.73	-	Converted to push/pull DSO 6111
2625	.53	.73	-	Converted to push/pull SO 6326
2626†$	.53	.72	-	Converted to push/pull DSO 6102
2627	.53	.72	-	Converted to push/pull SO 6313
2628†£	.53	.73	-	Converted to push/pull CSO 6210
2629	.53	.73	-	Converted to push/pull SO 6328
2630†£	.53	.73	-	Converted to push/pull CSO 6206
2631	.53	.72	?	Mullingar Scrapyard
2632†	.53	.72	-	Converted to push/pull CSO 6202
2633	.53	.72	?	Mullingar Scrapyard
2634†	.53	.73	-	Converted to push/pull DSO 6106
2635$	.53	.73	-	Converted to push/pull SO 6330
2636†	.53	.72	?	Mullingar Scrapyard
2637§	.53	.72	-	Converted to push/pull SO 6314
2638†	.53	.72	-	Converted to push/pull DSO 6105
2639	.53	.72	-	Converted to push/pull SO 6310
2640†	.53	.73	-	Converted to push/pull DSO 6107
2641§	.53	.72	-	Converted to push/pull SO 6317
2642†*	.53	.75	?	Mullingar Scrapyard
2643*	.53	.73	-	Converted to push/pull CSO 6211
2644†£	.53	.73	-	Converted to push/pull CSO 6209
2645+	.53	.72	-	Converted to push/pull SO 6303
2646†*	.53	.71	-	Converted to push/pull DSO 6101
2647+	.54	.71	-	Converted to push/pull SO 6301

2612 was destroyed by fire at Multyfarnham in August 1957.

DRIVING MOTOR BRAKE THIRD (*§ DRIVING MOTOR THIRD).

Built: 1954 by AEC/Park Royal Vehicles, London.
Engines: Two AEC of 250 hp (186 kW).
Transmission: Mechanical. SCG 5 speed gearbox.
Seats: 78 (* 94, §96, + 80).   **Length:** 62 ft 6 in (19.05 m).
Width: 9 ft 6 in (2.90 m).   **Weight:** 38.5 tons.
Brakes: Vacuum.

† Fitted with Clarkson Vapour boiler. Later replaced by Spanner Swirlyflow boiler, dates unknown.

Vehicle No.	Month to Traffic	Month Withdrawn	Month Cut Up	Disposal Location
2648†	.54	.75	?	Mullingar Scrapyard
2649*	.54	.73	-	Converted to push/pull SO 6332
2650†	.54	.73	-	Converted to push/pull CSO 6208
2651*	.54	.75	?	Mullingar Scrapyard
2652†	.54	.73	-	Converted to push/pull CSO 6207
2653*	.54	.73	-	Converted to push/pull SO 6322
2654†	.54	.75	?	Mullingar Scrapyard
2655*	.54	.73	-	Converted to push/pull SO 6324
2656†	.54	.61	-	Converted to MS 2668 (qv)
2657*	.54	.72	-	Converted to push/pull SO 6311
2658† +	.54	.72	-	Converted to push/pull CSO 6205
2659§	.54	.73	-	Converted to push/pull SO 6329

2658 & 2659 were used exclusively on the isolated Waterford to Tramore line until its closure on 31.12.60.

DRIVING MOTOR BRAKE STANDARD (* DRIVING MOTOR STANDARD).

Built: 1956 by CIE at Inchicore Works, Dublin to a Bullied design.
Engines: Two AEC of 250 hp (186 kW).
Transmission: Mechanical. SCG 5 speed gearbox.
Seats: 52S (* 64S).   **Length:** 62 ft 6 in (19.05 m).
Width: 9 ft 6 in (2.90 m).   **Weight:**
Brakes: Vacuum.

The DMBSO vehicles were converted to MBS in 1961.
The DMSO vehicles were converted to MS in 1961.

Vehicle No.	Month to Traffic	Month Withdrawn	Month Cut Up	Disposal Location
2660	.57	.72	-	Converted to push/pull SO 6312
2661*	.57	.72	-	Converted to push/pull SO 6320
2662	.57	.72	-	Converted to push/pull SO 6319
2663*	.57	.72	-	Converted to push/pull SO 6305
2664	.57	.72	-	Converted to push/pull SO 6316
2665*	.57	.72	-	Converted to push/pull SO 6307

MOTOR STANDARD (NON DRIVING)

Built: 1961 by CIE at Inchicore Works, Dublin.
Engines: Two AEC of 250 hp (186 kW).
Transmission: Mechanical. SCG 5 speed gearbox.
Seats: 52 (* 64).   **Length:** 62 ft 6 in (19.05 m).
Width: 9 ft 6 in (2.90 m).   **Weight:**
Brakes: Vacuum.

Converted from DMBCO vehicles 2614, 2617 & 2656 respectively, built 1952–54.

Vehicle No.	Month to Traffic	Month Withdrawn	Month Cut Up	Disposal Location
2666	.61	.73	-	Converted to push/pull SO 6321
2667*	.61	.72	-	Converted to push/pull SO 6315
2668	.61	.72	-	Converted to push/pull SO 6308

APPENDIX 2 - FORMER CIE PUSH/PULL VEHICLES

Note: The author recognises that much information is still required to make this section as complete as the rest of the book. If any readers can help with any of the missing information please contact the author at the publishers address for inclusion in future editions.

It should be noted that some of these vehicles were reseated on a number of occasions and full details are not available.

CIE/PARK ROYAL — DRIVING OPEN STANDARD

Built: 1971–73 by CIE at Inchicore Works, Dublin. Converted from former multiple unit stock built 1951–53.
Seats: 58.
Brakes: Vacuum.
Weight: 30 tons.
Bogies: AEC Design.
Length: 62 ft 6 in (19.05 m).
Width: 9 ft 6 in (2.90 m).

Vehicle No.	Ex DMU Number	Month Converted	Date Withdrawn	Month Cut Up	Disposal Location
6101	2646	.71	?	?	Mullingar Scrapyard
6102	2626	.72	21.10.74	?	Mullingar Scrapyard
6103	2618	.72	26.10.83	?	Mullingar Scrapyard
6104	2608	.72	?	?	Mullingar Scrapyard
6105	2638	.72	.02.83	06.83	Mullingar Scrapyard
6106	2634	.73	.84	?	Mullingar Scrapyard
6107	2640	.73	14.09.87	07.89	Dundalk
6108	2604	.73	06.03.82	06.83	Mullingar Scrapyard
6109	2600	.73	02.03.81	?	Mullingar Scrapyard
6110	2622	.73	.84	?	Mullingar Scrapyard
6111	2624	.73	14.09.87	-	Inchicore Works
6112	2620	.73	26.03.80	?	Mullingar Scrapyard

6101 & 6104 were both withdrawn following fire damage, date unknown.
6102 was withdrawn following an accident at Gormanston on 21.10.74.

CIE/PARK ROYAL — CONNECTOR OPEN STANDARD

Built: 1971–73 by CIE at Inchicore Works, Dublin. Converted from former multiple unit stock built 1951–54.
Seats: 58.
Brakes: Vacuum.
Weight: 30 tons.
Bogies: AEC Design.
Length: 62 ft 6 in (19.05 m).
Width: 9 ft 6 in (2.90 m).

Vehicle No.	Ex DMU Number	Month Converted	Date Withdrawn	Month Cut Up	Disposal Location
6201	2606	.71	26.10.83	?	Mullingar Scrapyard
6202	2632	.72	26.10.83	?	Mullingar Scrapyard
6203	2602	.72	14.09.87	?	Mullingar Scrapyard
6204	2610	.72	.84	?	Mullingar Scrapyard
6205	2658	.72	26.10.83	?	Mullingar Scrapyard
6206	2630	.73	14.09.87	07.89	Dundalk
6207	2652	.73	26.10.83	?	Mullingar Scrapyard
6208	2650	.73	.84	?	Mullingar Scrapyard
6209	2644	.73	26.10.83	?	Mullingar Scrapyard
6210	2628	.73	18.04.83	?	Mullingar Scrapyard
6211	2643	.73	.84	?	Mullingar Scrapyard
6212	2616	.73	.84	?	Mullingar Scrapyard

CIE/PARK ROYAL   OPEN STANDARD

Built: 1971–73 by CIE at Inchicore Works, Dublin. Converted from former multiple unit stock built 1951–54.
Seats: 70.
Brakes: Vacuum.
Weight: 30 tons.
Bogies: AEC Design.
Length: 62 ft 6 in (19.05 m).
Width: 9 ft 6 in (2.90 m).

Vehicle No.	Ex DMU Number	Month Converted	Date Withdrawn	Month Cut Up	Disposal Location
6301	2647	.71	26.10.83	?	Mullingar Scrapyard
6302	2605	.72	. .84	?	Mullingar Scrapyard
6303	2645	.72	15.12.81	?	Mullingar Scrapyard
6304	2621	.72	26.10.83	?	Mullingar Scrapyard

CIE/PARK ROYAL   OPEN STANDARD

Built: 1972 by CIE at Inchicore Works, Dublin. Converted from former multiple unit stock built 1956.
Seats: 66.
Brakes: Vacuum.
Weight: 30 tons.
Bogies: AEC Design.
Length: 62 ft 6 in (19.05 m).
Width: 9 ft 6 in (2.90 m).

Vehicle No.	Ex DMU Number	Month Converted	Date Withdrawn	Month Cut Up	Disposal Location
6305	2663	.72	. .84	?	Mullingar Scrapyard

CIE/PARK ROYAL   OPEN STANDARD

Details as 6301–4.

Vehicle No.	Ex DMU Number	Month Converted	Date Withdrawn	Month Cut Up	Disposal Location
6306	2619	.72	20.09.83	?	Mullingar Scrapyard

CIE/PARK ROYAL   OPEN STANDARD

Details as 6305.

Vehicle No.	Ex DMU Number	Month Converted	Date Withdrawn	Month Cut Up	Disposal Location
6307	2665	.72	. .84	?	Mullingar Scrapyard

CIE/PARK ROYAL   OPEN STANDARD

Built: 1972–73 by CIE at Inchicore Works, Dublin. Converted from former multiple unit stock built 1952–4.
Seats: 66.
Brakes: Vacuum.
Weight: 30 tons.
Bogies: AEC Design.
Length: 62 ft 6 in (19.05 m).
Width: 9 ft 6 in (2.90 m).

Vehicle No.	Ex DMU Number	Month Converted	Date Withdrawn	Month Cut Up	Disposal Location
6308	2668	.72	10.08.82	?	Mullingar Scrapyard

CIE/PARK ROYAL

OPEN STANDARD

Details as 6301–4.

Vehicle No.	Ex DMU Number	Month Converted	Date Withdrawn	Month Cut Up	Disposal Location
6309	2607	.72	12.09.83	?	Mullingar Scrapyard
6310	2639	.72	. .84	?	Mullingar Scrapyard
6311	2657	.72	14.09.87	07.89	Dundalk

CIE/PARK ROYAL

OPEN STANDARD

Details as 6305.

Vehicle No.	Ex DMU Number	Month Converted	Date Withdrawn	Month Cut Up	Disposal Location
6312	2660	.72	. .84	?	Mullingar Scrapyard

CIE/PARK ROYAL

OPEN STANDARD

Details as 6301–4.

Vehicle No.	Ex DMU Number	Month Converted	Date Withdrawn	Month Cut Up	Disposal Location
6313	2627	.72	. .84	?	Mullingar Scrapyard
6314	2637	.72	. .84	?	Mullingar Scrapyard

CIE/PARK ROYAL

OPEN STANDARD

Details as 6308.

Vehicle No.	Ex DMU Number	Month Converted	Date Withdrawn	Month Cut Up	Disposal Location
6315	2667	.72	. .84	?	Mullingar Scrapyard

CIE/PARK ROYAL

OPEN STANDARD

Details as 6305.

Vehicle No.	Ex DMU Number	Month Converted	Date Withdrawn	Month Cut Up	Disposal Location
6316	2664	.72	14.09.87	?	Mullingar Scrapyard

CIE/PARK ROYAL

OPEN STANDARD

Details as 6301–4.

Vehicle No.	Ex DMU Number	Month Converted	Date Withdrawn	Month Cut Up	Disposal Location
6317	2641	.72	15.12.82	?	Mullingar Scrapyard
6318	2615	.72	15.12.82	?	Mullingar Scrapyard

CIE/PARK ROYAL

OPEN STANDARD

Details as 6305.

Vehicle No.	Ex DMU Number	Month Converted	Date Withdrawn	Month Cut Up	Disposal Location
6319	2662	.72	. .84	?	Mullingar Scrapyard
6320	2661	.72	20.09.83	?	Mullingar Scrapyard

CIE/PARK ROYAL   OPEN STANDARD

Details as 6308.

Vehicle No.	Ex DMU Number	Month Converted	Date Withdrawn	Month Cut Up	Disposal Location
6321	2666	.73	26.10.83	?	Mullingar Scrapyard

CIE/PARK ROYAL   OPEN STANDARD

Details as 6301–4.

Vehicle No.	Ex DMU Number	Month Converted	Date Withdrawn	Month Cut Up	Disposal Location
6322	2653	.73	. .84	?	Dundalk
6323	2613	.73	26.10.83	?	Mullingar Scrapyard
6324	2655	.73	02.04.82	06.83	Mullingar Scrapyard
6325	2611	.73	20.11.82	06.83	Mullingar Scrapyard
6326	2625	.73	16.02.82	?	Mullingar Scrapyard
6327	2609	.73	. .86	?	Mullingar Scrapyard
6328	2629	.73	. .84	?	Mullingar Scrapyard
6329	2659	.73	. .84	?	Mullingar Scrapyard
6330	2635	.73	26.10.83	?	Mullingar Scrapyard
6331	2623	.73	. .84	?	Mullingar Scrapyard
6332	2649	.73	. .84	?	Mullingar Scrapyard

APPENDIX 3 - DISPOSAL OF ASBESTOS CON-TAMINATED VEHICLES

In the late 1970s new regulations were introduced controlling the handling and disposal of asbestos contaminated vehicles which had previously been broken up without special precautions. The two railway companies were faced with the problem of disposing of many redundant vehicles which were found to contain blue asbestos between the outer and inner skins of the vehicle bodies and roofs. Neither of the two companies possessed the special facilities required by law to dispose of these contaminated vehicles and therefore a feasibility study was undertaken by NIR, (who owned most of the affected vehicles), to decide the safest and most economic way to resolve the problem. Six different schemes were explored, each of which is detailed below, together with the final reccommendations made.

Scheme A - Shallow Water Disposal.

This scheme involved the transportation of the vehicles from either Stormont Wharf or Albert Quay by ship to Beaufort Dyke, which is 8 to 10 miles east north east of the Copeland Islands, for dumping at sea. However, the Water Pollution Control Branch at Stormont reported that dumping was not possible under the Oslo Convention Annexe 2, in that bulky material cannot be dumped on the Continental Shelf. Any dumping at sea must be in water at least 6000 feet deep and must be at least 150 miles from the nearest land.

Scheme B - Stripping at Antrim Goods Yard.

This scheme involved the dismantling of the affected vehicles under controlled conditions by outside contractors at the former goods yard at Antrim. The cost of providing the special facilities required by law, including the construction of a sealed building in which the eventual stripping of the asbestos would take place, proved to be too expensive and the whole scheme was found to be too long and complex.

Scheme C - Deep water disposal.

Following the conclusions reached in scheme A, the possibility of deep water dumping of the vehicles was explored. However, the application was refused by the Department of the Environment as alternative land based methods were available.

Scheme D - Burning under controlled circumstances.

No facilities existed for the controlled burning of contaminated vehicles in Ireland and the nearest available licensed facility was that at the premises of King & Sons Ltd., Newmarket (now Mayer Newman Ltd.). The possibility of transporting these vehicles by sea from Belfast to Felixstowe and then conveying them by rail to Newmarket was explored, but the different track and loading gauges precluded this option. An alternative option of conveying the vehicles by road on low loaders from Felixstowe was found to be impracticable as road access to the yard was limited. The cost of sea transport was also very high and therefore this scheme was abandoned.

Scheme E - Burial in abandoned tunnel.

The abandoned Lisummon Tunnel on the former route from Markethill to Goraghwood was found to be in a satisfactory condition following an inspection by the permanent way department. Reinstatement of the line for the short distance from Goraghwood to the tunnel mouth was planned so that the vehicles could be delivered directly to the site. Upon completion the tunnel mouths would be plugged with concrete and the line back to Goraghwood lifted. This scheme met with approval, but scheme F below ultimately was found to be more cost effective and required little capital outlay.

Section F - Burial in Crosshill Quarry, Co. Antrim.

The scheme ultimately adopted. The former quarry at Crosshill, Co. Antrim was found to be an ideal site for the burial of the contaminated vehicles, being only a short distance from the railway line at Crumlin. The vehicles were "Shrink wrapped" at York Road prior to delivery to a specially laid siding at Crumlin station for final transportation by road to the quarry. The quarry was partially filled with water, with depths varying between 40 and 80 feet. In addition to the vehicles shown in the text, the following CIE vehicles were also dumped in the quarry in February 1985: 1497, 1498, 1499, 1500, 1631, 1924, 1925, 1927, 1929, 1930, 2402.

APPENDIX 4 - ACCOMMODATION.

Belfast

"Helga Lodge", Cromwell Road, Botanic, Belfast.   Belfast 324820

Directions: Turn left outside Botanic station and continue for approx. 100 metres. Turn second left into Cromwell Road and "Helga Lodge" is almost immediately on the right hand side. (Walking time less than 5 minutes).

Cork

"Oaklands", 51 Lower Glanmire Road, Cork.   Cork 500578

Directions: Turn right outside the main station gates and proceed along Lower Glanmire Road for approx. 100 metres. "Oaklands" is on the right hand side (Walking time less than 5 minutes).

"Tivoli House", 143 Lower Glanmire Road, Cork.   Cork 506605

Directions: Turn right outside the main station gates and proceed along Lower Glanmire Road for approx. 400 metres. "Tivoli House" is on the left hand side, just before the railway bridge. (Walking time 5 minutes).

Drogheda

"Georgian Door", Dublin Road, Drogheda.   Drogheda 38517

Directions: Turn right outside the station and follow the main road down the hill for approx. 500 metres. "Georgian Door" is on the left hand side. (Walking time 10 minutes).

Dublin

"Elmar Hotel", 34 Gardiner Street, Dublin.   Dublin 741246

Directions: Leave Connolly Station by the steps from the main concourse, cross Amiens Street, and proceed down Talbot Street for approx. 300 metres. Turn 2nd right in to Gardiner Street & "Elmar Hotel" is on the left hand side. (Walking time 10 minutes).

"Tipperary House", 7 Parkgate Street, Dublin.   Dublin 795317

Directions: Leave Heuston Station by the Bus pick up/set down exit. Turn first left and cross the River Liffey, and then right. Fork immediately left into Parkgate Street and continue for approx. 200 metres. "Tipperary House" is on the left hand side. (Walking time 5 minutes).

"Kingsbridge", 14 Parkgate Street, Dublin.   Dublin 773263

Directions: Leave Heuston Station by the Bus pick up/set down exit. Turn first left and cross the River Liffey. "Kingsbridge" is almost directly opposite across Parkgate Street. (Walking time less than 5 minutes).

"Wellington House", 20 Conyngham Road, Dublin.   Dublin 713043

Directions: Leave Heuston Station by the Bus pick up/set down exit. Turn first left across the River Liffey and then left into Parkgate Street. Continue into Conyngham Road and "Wellington House" is on the left hand side approx. 200 metres past the bus depot. (Walking time 10 minutes).

Limerick

"Boylans", 22 Davis Street, Limerick.   Limerick 48916

Directions: Leave the station by the main exit and cross the main road. Proceed along Davis Street and "Boylans"is approx. 100 metres further along on the right. (Walking time less than 5 minutes).

Waterford

"Lonegans", The Quays, Waterford.   Waterford 75198

Directions: Leave the station by the main exit and cross the River Suir. Turn first left along The Quayside and "Lonegans" is approx. 100 metres further along on the right hand side. (Walking time 5 minutes).